T0093575

# Intelligent Safety

# Intelligent Safety

How to Protect Your **Connected Family** from **Big Cybercrime**

**HARI RAVICHANDRAN**

Foreword by Jeffrey Katzenberg

Skyhorse Publishing

Skyhorse Publishing books may be purchased in bulk at special discounts for sales promotion, corporate gifts, fund-raising, or educational purposes. Special editions can also be created to specifications. For details, contact the Special Sales Department, Skyhorse Publishing, 307 West 36th Street, 11th Floor, New York, NY 10018 or info@skyhorsepublishing.com.

Skyhorse® and Skyhorse Publishing® are registered trademarks of Skyhorse Publishing, Inc.®, a Delaware corporation.

Visit our website at www.skyhorsepublishing.com.

10 9 8 7 6 5 4 3 2 1

Library of Congress Cataloging-in-Publication Data is available on file.

Cover design by Kajya Arndt-Truong

ISBN: 978-1-5107-7496-4
Ebook ISBN: 978-1-5107-7578-7

Printed in the United States of America

# Contents

# Foreword

## The Next Big Thing in Digital Safety
### by Jeffrey Katzenberg

When I sold DreamWorks Animation in 2016, I woke up the next day and asked myself: *If you were twenty-three and starting your career, what would you be doing?* The answer was simple. I would be living in Silicon Valley and working in digital technology.

The role and impact that technology has played in every facet of our lives over this past decade has been monumental. I believe this will be even greater over the next decade. The possibilities are exciting and there are many brilliant entrepreneurs with phenomenal ideas that I'm confident will revolutionize many industries and I want to be a part of that revolution.

There's no question that technology can improve our lives for the better, but unfortunately, that convenience also comes with risks. Particularly when it comes to our security. By living so much of our lives online, we're putting ourselves and our families at risk, and most of us don't even realize it.

We have all gone to great lengths to protect our homes. Alarm systems, cameras, and advanced doorbells provide the highest level of physical security. Consumers around the globe are expected to spend nearly $100 billion on home security by 2028. But, if thieves broke into your home, what could they take? Some electronics, TVs, computers, and jewelry, and likely very little cash, so the actual monetary damage of what can be stolen is limited.

Now consider the assets that are accessible through your phone. I know for a fact that a thief could do significantly more financial damage with access to my phone than to my home. Credit cards, bank accounts, Social Security number, almost all my most important information is on my phone or in the cloud, so it's no surprise that in 2020, for the first time ever, the American financial loss from online crime surpassed that from home burglaries: $3.3 billion versus $2.7 billion, according to the FTC[1] and FBI.[2] In that year alone, there was a 70 percent increase in internet crime, according to the FBI's Internet Crime Report.

In 2021, that number doubled to $6.9 billion stolen.[3]

Stats like this make me feel incredibly vulnerable, and you can be sure that these numbers will only worsen.

When I look back at my tech habits, I get embarrassed. I'd go as far as to call myself a digital dummy.

Although I have benefited immensely from technology throughout my career, I know little about it. I had all the latest security devices to protect my home and my physical world, but I wasn't doing the same for my digital life. It was as though I was putting three locks and bolting the front door while leaving the back door wide open.

That's why I was excited to partner up with people who had the knowledge and experience. It's how I came to work closely with Hari Ravichandran and Aura, who have tackled the digital crime crisis head-on by creating an entirely new category of digital security called intelligent safety, which leverages AI to help digital dummies like me stay a step ahead of increasingly sophisticated criminals. They've built a product from the ground up that was designed for the family and puts my mind at ease.

I've played many roles throughout my career; they all revolve around storytelling, and I don't see this next opportunity being any different. Consumers need to understand the magnitude of the problem they face online and how vulnerable they can be, but they also need to know that there is a solution. I believe that is the next big story that needs to be told, and there is nobody better than Hari to tell it.

# Preface

## Finally, a Proactive Solution

The home loan I applied for in 2014 should have been simple. I didn't give it a second thought, which is why I was so shocked when it was denied due to poor credit. I hadn't been monitoring my credit closely, but I didn't have to. I made a decent income, hadn't made any large purchases, and always paid my bills in full and on time. This had to be a mistake . . . except it wasn't.

When I looked into the issue, I realized that my credit score had plummeted, but it wasn't because of anything I had done. Someone had stolen my identity and, among other things, tried to take out a mortgage in my name. I had no idea who this person was, yet they had obtained the most personal information about me. It was unsettling, and my mind raced with questions. *What other damage had been done? How did they get this information? Were my kids and family impacted? Was I still at risk, and could something like this, or worse, happen again?*

I couldn't relax until I figured out how the breach had occurred and how to prevent something like it from ever happening again. But there was no simple way for me to dig in and find out what happened and there definitely wasn't an easy solution to my problem. In fact, my search generated many more questions than answers. The market was saturated with dozens of products designed to address only certain parts of the problem. There was antivirus software, ransomware prevention, credit monitoring, transaction monitoring, Wi-Fi security, password managers, and dark web scanning to name just a few.

A lot of companies offered a lot of solutions, but I had no clue which ones were best or even which ones I needed. And, even if I decided to cobble together all of these resources, it would cost me a couple hundred dollars a month and still wouldn't give me everything I needed, because the resources weren't personalized. Most of these solutions were not easy to use. They were one-size-fits-all solutions that didn't consider the details of my online life, which left lots of room for things to slip in through the cracks.

What was most noticeable was that these solutions would sound alarm bells to notify me when my information was stolen again, but they didn't actually prevent my information from being stolen in the first place. They didn't address my bigger concern—protecting my family.

The whole process of looking for the right solution to remedy the damage done when I was hacked proved to be a complex, expensive, and frustrating headache. And I couldn't have been the only one who felt that way. This problem wasn't going away, so somebody needed to solve it. As an engineer and entrepreneur who had already built successful start-ups, I saw an opportunity to do just that. By marrying my ability to solve massive problems with cutting-edge technology, I could make this journey much easier for families.

I refused to believe that there wasn't a solution to the problem of digital safety. People shouldn't have to experience what

I did. I became determined to fill the gap in the market by using technology to create a service that would allow everyone to live freely and safely online.

That was the birth of Aura, but this book doesn't tell my story, and it's not a sales pitch. Any service I write about in these pages could easily be outdated by the time the book is published. The point of this book is to lay the groundwork so you can better understand how to protect yourself and your family online. To put you in control.

When I set out on this journey, I first needed to understand how the problem of digital safety evolved, and that's the focus of part 1. I explain how cybercrime works and how the types of scams you can fall victim to are only increasing as we live more and more online. Everything is available at our fingertips today, but that convenience requires us to share more of our personal information than ever before. That data is extremely valuable, so if you aren't careful and don't know how to protect your information, you're not only putting your money and credit at risk but also your reputation, peace of mind, and your family's safety.

At Aura, we are committed to making intelligent safety accessible to all. Intelligent safety describes the predictive, proactive, personalized protection that empowers families to confidently navigate their increasingly complex digital lives. It is an easy-to-use digital guardian that won't force you to compromise any of the modern conveniences you've grown used to. But at its heart is AI that anticipates threats before they happen—instantly blocking a malicious link found in a text message, turning on Wi-Fi protection when using public Wi-Fi, or automatically changing passwords that it finds on the dark web. It continually learns and adapts to each individual to better understand how that user might be at risk, so it can personalize protection.

This vision to create a safer internet is the focus of part 2. It's about how we can use technology to create protection that is more than the sum of its parts. Technology that moves us beyond reactive alarms that only alert you when a problem arises, but instead automates the steps to provide proactive preventative protection. Intelligent safety is most effective because it considers and personalizes protections for the actions of each individual; it does not only apply one-size-fits-all security to your devices.

Knowledge and awareness are half of the battle, and there are preventative protections you can implement today. I lay out those tools and best practices and actions you can take. Whether safeguarding your devices; shielding your kids from harmful content, cyberbullying and predators; keeping your aging parents out of harm's way from targeted scams; or securing your family finances, you can take back control of your life.

That's what I set out to achieve in this book. Because, the lagging impact of a hack can stay with you for years. I was lucky that it only took me a couple of months to ensure all of my accounts were secure, but I didn't get off completely scot-free. Eight years later, I still have to go to my local IRS office every year when I file my tax return just to prove that I am who I say I am. I've gotten to know some of the employees very well, and they've been great to me, but still, it's a trip I'd rather not have to make.

Cybercriminals prey on fear and urgency. They exploit those who don't understand the digital landscape and trust that their devices are safe and secure. By understanding how people put themselves at risk and changing risky online behavior while implementing simple proactive practices, you can give yourself the peace of mind of knowing that you and your family are protected.

# PART 1
# How Intelligent Safety Can Stop Big Cybercrime

Cybercriminals target specific people in ways that are much more likely to bypass those one-size-fits-all solutions, which is why cybercrime is the fastest growing crime in the United States.[1] A total of $6.9 billion was lost to internet crime in 2021. That's up from $4.1 billion in 2020, which is a 68 percent increase in one year alone.[2] It's had such an impact on the global economy that cybersecurity has now become part of the President's Daily Brief.

When you leave the house, you lock your door. When you get into the car, you put on your seat belt. But when we venture into the digital world, most of us don't employ those same precautions. Why? The simple reason is that most people never develop the proper habits because they don't know how they are exposed online.

In the 1990s, the closest thing we had to a digital transaction was calling an 800 number to purchase something from an infomercial. That's back when we thought of hackers as a bunch of overgrown kids living in their parents' basements targeting corporations and ripping people off for a couple hundred bucks. They were the only ones with the technological know-how to pull something like that off.

In the early 2000s, we saw a shift from hackers targeting organizations to targeting everyday people through a series of viruses and computer worms that attacked common software programs, such as those from Microsoft. That got people to realize the internet could be used as a weapon of mass destruction, but many of these early cyberattacks were stunts. The perpetrators were more interested in notoriety and wreaking havoc than profit.

By 2010, profit-driven attacks using malware and ransomware gained in popularity with the advent of Bitcoin, a hard-to-trace currency that hackers used to demand payment and reduce the risk that they'd ever be caught. The world continues to change rapidly, and as more aspects of our lives switch from the real world to the online world, we've reached a new inflection point when it comes to digital crime, and it's centered around our data.

I can finance and purchase a car with a mobile app, pay my utility bill online, have a doctor's appointment via Zoom, and open my garage door from halfway around the world. This makes life convenient, but even the simplest digital transactions, such as ordering food from DoorDash or Uber Eats, require our information to be transferred multiple times. We're spending more time and buying more things online than ever. That only increases the size of our digital footprint, which means we're putting so much personal information out there that we might as well post it on a billboard. That data has become valuable because it can be used to steal our identity and hack into our accounts.

In the meantime, the basement hackers have been replaced by organized criminal institutions. This includes the scam call centers you've heard about and have probably received calls from. They are just some of the groups who operate like a business to exploit digital weaknesses and scam people out of money. They have a tremendous amount of resources and technological skill, but the tools we're using to protect ourselves online were built for the basement hacker on a desktop computer with a dial-up modem. They were designed to prevent the worms and viruses those turn-of-the-century hackers unleashed on the public. They never anticipated the advancements that we'd make in personal technology in a few short years. That leaves our families more vulnerable to complex modern cyberattacks, and without the proper protections, we don't stand a chance.

Today, the average family has dozens of digital accounts and an estimated twenty-five connected devices in their homes.[3] Believe it or not, your baby cam, refrigerator, dishwasher, car, toys, and printer can all be potential access points to your digital world that criminals can exploit.

When these devices are not updated and upgraded, they can all become potential vulnerabilities and points of entry for bad actors. More devices and more convenience create more vulnerabilities that make your family susceptible to more digital threats. As technology becomes more sophisticated, so do cybercriminals. Cybercriminals today can take money out of your 401(k) and file a second mortgage on your house without you ever knowing anything about it.

Some people feel that digital safety is an oxymoron and that we don't ever have a chance of being secure online, but I refuse to believe that. The first step to becoming more protected and making the internet safer for you and your family is becoming more digitally literate. To do that, you must first understand cybercrime, how it works, and how you can be targeted.

# CHAPTER 1

# The Business of Cybercrime

It was a typical Friday. Lauren got up right when her alarm went off at 6:30 a.m. The day began like every weekday, but this would be the day she learned just how vulnerable her family was. It would completely change the way they thought about security.

Before even getting out of bed, the first thing Lauren always did was check her phone, but on this day, she didn't have any cell service. No bars at all. Cell service had been spotty before, usually never at home, but she didn't think anything of it and went about her day.

When she finished making breakfast for the kids, she instinctively picked up her phone again. Still no service. She checked her husband's phone when he came downstairs. He had service, which was strange because they both had AT&T and were on the same plan, so it wasn't like she had forgotten to pay the bill. Something was up.

Lauren used her husband's phone to call AT&T. Once she finally got a human on the line, she was told her account had been switched to T-Mobile. *What? That doesn't make any sense!* It sounded like a bizarre mix-up on their end, but the rep insisted that he couldn't help her and that she needed to contact T-Mobile for more information.

More confused than concerned, she phoned T-Mobile. This customer service rep could confirm her account had been transferred from AT&T, but he couldn't tell her anything else since she didn't have the proper PIN or any of the account setup information. This wasn't a mistake. This was intentional. Someone else had done this.

Now in a full-blown panic, Lauren and her husband knew something was wrong. They just didn't know what. It had to be some kind of fraud, but what was the scam, and how did this happen? They had antivirus software and credit monitoring. They kept their personal information and account numbers private. They knew not to click strange links and stopped answering spam phone calls long ago. As far as they knew, they were protected.

After doing some research online, they learned Lauren was the victim of a SIM swap; a scam where the criminal poses as the victim to call their cell provider and reroute service to another carrier. That meant the scammer now had complete control of her phone. All they needed to do was restore the most recent cloud backup of Lauren's phone to access all her text messages, photos, and the apps she used on that phone. That included her banking app. Once Lauren and her husband realized that, they immediately checked their account, and were shocked to find their savings, all $80,000, gone!

Lauren may not be a real person, but her story is far from fiction. It's inspired by the hundreds of calls Aura's fraud resolution teams receive daily. This happens all the time, but nobody sees it coming because they don't understand how vulnerable they really are. And I don't blame them. I didn't understand it either until it happened to me, and I didn't think it was possible because I thought I was protected.

Most people aren't reckless. They're careful with their information, so they assume their lives are safe, but they aren't as safe as they *need* to be because they don't associate certain behaviors with the seriousness of the potential problem that can occur on the back end.

We don't take the time to develop secure passwords, and we don't change them often. Worse, we use the same password for multiple accounts. We don't take the time to set up multifactor authentication because it's a pain. We know that it makes us more secure, but we don't want to be bothered because we don't understand how much this simple step can protect us and how much we are at risk without it. Besides, we assume that we're already protected. We cannot help but instinctively trust that the stewards of our information are looking out for our best interest and will keep us safe if something goes wrong. We believe that Apple or our PC provider will prevent our devices from being hacked and that if someone runs up a bunch of charges on our credit card, the credit card company will take care of that.

What Lauren and most people don't realize is that nobody is unhackable. It's shockingly easy for cybercriminals to access your data. In the physical world, we can assess any threats in our orbit simply by looking around, but the online world is a much different story. It's a different world with a different set of rules—one that too many people don't understand.

## Understanding the Digital Crime Landscape

Microsoft CEO Satya Nadella has called cybercrime the new pandemic because he believes it will live with us for years.

We're bombarded with stories about major corporations being hacked—Target, Sony, and Twitter. State-sponsored actors can engage in cyberwarfare to potentially shut down the power grid of an entire country. We read about these massive breaches that bankrupt companies and expose swaths of data so large that it's difficult to wrap our heads around what it even means. Major companies such as Yahoo, First American Financial Corporation, LinkedIn, Facebook, and dozens more experienced data breaches that exposed the personal information of billions of users yet paid no penalty for not protecting that data. The threat to government agencies and companies is enormous, but that's not what this book is about.

This book is about you and how you can protect yourself and your family. You may not think you're a target or that you are at risk, but you are in fact, the most vulnerable. There has been a lot of focus on enterprise security and its responsibility for taking care of consumer data. The federal government has regulated how big tech uses data. That's where most of the venture dollars go, but there's very little out there for the individual consumer. As a result, unfortunately, too many people are forced to learn the hard way (myself included) just how vulnerable they are, but it doesn't have to be that way.

Before you can improve your digital safety habits, you need to better understand the playing field, specifically the three layers of the internet: surface web, deep web, and dark web.

1. **Surface web:** This is every public website you can access—all 1.88 billion of them. If a site can be found through a search, it's on the surface web. However, it's estimated that we only spend about 10 percent of our time on the surface web.

2. **Deep web:** These are the sites that require a username and password to access. Email, banking, and social media are all on the deep web. If your bank's homepage is a public site on the surface web, the profile and personal information you can access with your username and password is on the deep web. For every public web page, there might be millions of pages on the deep web.

3. **Dark web:** This is where you go to be anonymous. Using peer-to-peer networks like Tor or Freenet, you access a series of encrypted networks to hide your location and identity. It's used by whistleblowers and journalists to protect their privacy. It was actually designed by the US intelligence community to share sensitive information, and yes, this is also exploited by criminals to commit fraud and buy and sell personal data.

When you hear of corporate hacks and data breaches, the dark web is where that information is gathered and put up for sale. It's where criminals go to get the data required to access your personal information on the deep web. And this data is available in droves. Hackers can go on the dark web to buy identities and credit numbers. Access to someone's entire online identity is worth around $1,000.[1] Full identities, account information, and credit card numbers can also be bought in bulk—packages that total millions. There is a good chance your data is on there, and can include, but is not limited to:

- **Personal:** Name, address, birth date, phone number, Social Security number, and email address.
- **Financial:** Credit card information, banking and investment account information, insurance records, cryptocurrency accounts, and even information about cash payment apps such as Venmo.
- **Login:** Compromised username and password combinations to various accounts and services.
- **Medical:** Medical documents, insurance information, prescription history, billing information, and even biometric data such as fingerprints and images of your face.
- **Corporate:** Classified information, patents, operational details, and intellectual property.
- **Forged:** Phony passports, driver's licenses, bank drafts, and more.

And everything is for sale. The fact that there is such a thing called the Dark Web Price Index where you can see the going rate for this stolen information is a clear indication how normal this practice has become. It lists everything from a hacked Uber account for $4 to a credit card with a $1,000 balance for only $150. It's scary how easily this information can be acquired for such little cost.

Once you know the tools of the trade and how cybercriminals acquire large quantities of data, you need to know how they plan to use it. Some attacks are sophisticated, and others mind-numbingly simple. Either way, you want to know what to look out for.

## What Is Cybercrime, and How Does It Work?

Cybercrime takes on many forms and is conducted by a host of actors; some are lone individuals but most are part of larger organized networks. These are located around the world, many in countries where they can more freely operate outside the law. They can have cartel-like infrastructure. Some resemble legitimate sales operations, right down to employees working in call center environments trying to hit certain targets so they can move up the ladder. They have days off and even take vacations. That's the reason why we see a dip in phishing attacks on the weekends and during certain times of the year.

Cybercrime has become an ecosystem. Some organizations specialize in specific scams, which allows them to create sophisticated attacks and hone them over time. People within those organizations can each have their own area of expertise. Some may specialize in technology. Others may build malware. Some might focus on what to do with the money and data once it's been stolen. They are knowledgeable, resourceful, and motivated to get your money, but they don't need much information to make you a target. Sometimes all they need are the basics:

- Full name
- Current address
- Birthday
- Email address
- Phone number

This information can be found without any hacking or purchasing of data. Whether you realize it or not, it's probably already out there. Don't believe me? Take a minute to Google your name and your address or phone number. You will most likely see that all this information, along with that of all your family members, is listed on data brokerage sites. If, by some miracle, you aren't listed, congratulations! That's incredibly rare.

This information is used to commit fraud, and one of the most common forms of cybercrime—identity theft. In 2021, the Federal Trade Commission (FTC) received 1.4 million reports of identity theft.[2] Cybercriminals will often steal your identity to go after your finances. That means accessing and taking over your bank and credit card accounts. They can take out a mortgage or loans in your name, but that's not all. What's so frightening is that fraud comes in so many forms and can impact people in many ways. Some common examples include:

## Medical Fraud

Criminals can use your identity, insurance information, medical records, and Medicare number to receive medical services and prescription drugs in your name. This can alter your medical history, and can result in you possibly receiving an incorrect or dangerous diagnosis. It can also be expensive to clean up. Two-thirds of all victims report losing more than $13,500 due to fraudulent bills.[3]

## Employment Fraud

If criminals have a record and want to avoid background checks, or aren't legally allowed to work in the United States, they might apply for a job in your name. Multiple employee records can impact your credit, taxes, and Social Security benefits.

Scammers can also claim unemployment benefits in your name using your driver's license or Social Security number, and then change the address or bank account information to their own, so you aren't initially aware your identity was stolen. This type of crime is on the rise. The U.S. Department of Labor reported that between March and October 2021, up to $5.4 billion in unemployment benefits might have been stolen due to fraud.[4]

## Criminal Identity Theft

Just like criminals might use your information to get a job, they can also use it to avoid arrest by giving law enforcement your information instead of theirs, and guess whose record that goes on? This can result in outstanding traffic violations, court summons, warrants for your arrest, or in the case of Nicole McCabe, much worse.[5]

McCabe was an Australian living in Tel Aviv, and one of three people whose identity was stolen by the assassins of a high-ranking Hamas official in Dubai. If that wasn't bad enough, she was six months pregnant when she found out she was wanted for questioning. Just because you physically have your passport, driver's license, and Social Security card, doesn't mean that cybercriminals can't purchase that information online to create a clone of your documents, and travel the world under your name. McCabe and the others were quickly exonerated when authorities determined the photographs the assassins used to enter the country with the phony passports that were taken at customs didn't match the original authentic documents. In this case, the charges were so outrageous and the crime so extreme that authorities were able to determine that a pregnant woman was not an international assassin, but it's something nobody wants to experience.

## Tax Fraud

With access to your name, Social Security number, and birth-date, a cybercriminal can file taxes under your name. They typically report massive amounts of income to receive an equally massive refund. Don't underestimate this potential problem. In 2020, the IRS flagged 5.2 million tax returns as fraudulent.[6] If you think that's bad, the following year they reported a 91 percent increase in identity theft and tax fraud.[7]

So many of these issues are connected, so if scammers use your Social Security number and personal information when applying for a job, this can result in you getting tax documents from an employer you've never worked for. And that leads to reported income that is not your own. This requires you to work out this issue with the IRS and the Social Security Administration, which are not always user-friendly.

## Biometric Identity Theft

You know how your iPhone scans your face, so you don't need to type in a password? Well, they can steal that, too, along with the fingerprint identification required to get into your phone, laptop, digital wallets, and various bank accounts. On a larger scale, this data can be used to access secure office buildings and private company data. This occurs when companies storing this biometric data are breached.

## Credit Card Fraud

Roughly 127 million Americans have experienced credit card fraud. That's nearly half of all American adults. More than one in three of those adults has experienced multiple instances of card fraud. As with almost every other form of cybercrime, it's increased since the start of the pandemic, with a 44 percent spike between 2019 and 2020. The FTC estimates that $38 million was directly tied to COVID-19-related credit fraud.

Being a victim of credit fraud can impact other areas of your life. Depending on the size and nature of the fraud, it could negatively impact your credit score. That is reversible, but it can take months or even years to recover. However, if a scammer has other pieces of personal or financial information, they can be used to commit more attacks. Credit card fraud could quickly snowball into other forms of financial fraud and identity theft if you don't catch it and take action soon enough.

It isn't only the consumer who is hurt by this type of crime. When credit card companies refund fraudulent purchases, the business that provided the service or goods can also be impacted through chargeback fees. Big retailers can absorb the fees as part of the cost of doing business, but small businesses can be hobbled. They are much more vulnerable.

Credit card fraud is big business for criminal organizations, so they can devote a massive number of resources and manpower to getting your money. These scams can range from old-school grifter techniques, such as eyeing your PIN when you plug it into an ATM, to using technologically advanced keylogging software to capture your login information.

Credit card skimming is an example that requires a little more technical expertise to pull off, making it even more frightening. In this scam, thieves install devices inside legitimate card payment terminals to collect the data from the card's magnetic strip. ATMs and gas pumps are popular targets. Criminals use this to create a cloned card. When the card's magnetic strip was replaced with a chip, skimming was replaced by shimming (devices that read chips instead of the strip), proving that cybercrime will continually evolve with the technology.

## Deed Fraud

Not qualifying for a mortgage because your identity was stolen is bad, but losing the actual home where you live can be much worse. This type of fraud can occur when cybercriminals use your information to transfer the title of your home to another person. They can sell the home, rent it out, or steal the equity you've built up over time. This is deed fraud (or title fraud), and its victims tend to be older homeowners and those who own vacation homes.

Similar fake landlord scams can occur when someone loses their home to foreclosures but fails to inform the tenants and continues collecting rent. Sometimes scammers break into vacant homes, change the locks, and then either sell the homes or collect rent from victims. They have even been known to forge the owner's name on the deed to sell it to themselves and register the home in their name at the county recorder's office. That makes the home theirs on paper, and lets them take out a loan on the house, leaving the owner with the payments. It sounds outrageous, but with enough of your personal and financial information, scammers can do just about anything.

Sixty-five-year-old June Walker worked hard for two years to pay off her home on Detroit's east side in 2021.[8] She replaced the furnace, water heater, and the plumbing. Only two months later, she received an eviction letter. It turned out the property manager she had been paying was not the real property manager. He had created a fake deed and just stole her payments. This scam has become so common where June lives in Detroit that it's believed to affect one in ten tenants facing eviction. The foreclosure crisis and poor housing market make the area more susceptible to this type of scam because it's not always clear who owns these homes. What's frightening about these scams is that thieves don't even need your personal information to pull it off. The same is true about the next scam.

## Romance Scams

One of the most infamous examples of this can be found in the Netflix documentary *The Tinder Swindler*. Israeli Shimon Hayut posed as a wealthy businessman with a lavish lifestyle to attract unsuspecting women. He would wine and dine them using money he stole from other women, so he definitely looked and acted the part. Once he gained their trust, he would claim he was being targeted by his rivals and request loans and credit card information that he would use to bleed his victims dry. By the time he was apprehended, it's estimated that he stole $10 million. This isn't an isolated incident. In 2021, twenty-four thousand Americans were targeted in romance scams, resulting in more than $1 billion in theft.[9]

These types of romance scams have been around long before the internet, but they can occur more frequently in the digital age. Today, roughly 30 percent of Americans use a dating site or app—48 percent between the ages of eighteen and twenty-nine.[10] Younger people frequently use these apps, but this is also one of the biggest scams used to target seniors and older adults.

The Tinder Swindler is different in that he actually met with the women he targeted in person, but most scammers make it a point not to meet their intended victims. Instead, they string them along, claiming to be busy with work, or always traveling. They start by creating fake profiles, and often steal photos from social media or other dating profiles. Once they match with their target, they move the conversation off the platform and onto Snapchat, WhatsApp, or Telegram. They try to seduce their victims, gain their trust, and move the relationship forward quickly. That's when they try to get you to send them money, often for what they say is an emergency. But it's not always money they're after. Sometimes scammers will use dating sites to get you to give up sensitive personal information so they can hack your accounts and steal your identity.

## Synthetic Identity Theft

This is one of the worst-case scenarios that can occur and it involves scammers using stolen data to Frankenstein an entirely new fictional identity. It's a complicated process that involves creating an official record that the fictional person exists by applying for credit. Even when initially denied, they use that record to piggyback on legitimate accounts by being added as an authorized user. The end goal is to run up as much credit as possible and then disappear without a trace. Sometimes they can claim fraud and try to cash in twice on the phony accounts, but if your personal information is linked to those accounts, it's not just the banks and lenders that take a hit. Your credit can be impacted, and you can be vulnerable to a host of other attacks.

Synthetic identity theft is complicated but lucrative and much harder to detect. That's why it's one of the fastest-growing types of identity theft and makes up between 80 and 85 percent of all identity fraud, costing banks $20 billion in annual losses.[11]

Cybercriminals are resourceful, but they can't always find the information and data they need to conduct a hack online. Sometimes, they have to get it from other sources, and often the best source is you.

## Malware and Phishing Attacks

One of the easiest ways for scammers to gain access to your data is through malware. That's the name for malicious software, and it broadly includes viruses, spyware, adware, worms, Trojan horses, keyloggers, and ransomware that allow hackers to gain access to your devices through known vulnerabilities. It's an effective way to harvest your data, but different malware works in different ways. For example, keyloggers can intercept everything you type and click, including logins and passwords, even if you don't submit the information. These can be used by the hacker to gain access to your accounts, or they can be sold. Some malware takes a more direct approach to make money, such as ransomware that infects and encrypts your data, so you need to pay a ransom to retrieve it. Malware is just another tool of the trade that cybercriminals can buy and sell on the dark web.

Sometimes malware is disguised as advertising banners or illegal downloads, but one of the most common ways criminals attempt to plant malware on your computer is by getting you to click on links. This is the basis for what is known as phishing attacks, and we've all seen these. They are the robocalls, emails, and links sent to us that scream "scam!" These are the most common and, frankly, the laziest, which is why they're called spray-and-pray attacks. Criminals blast these links out to thousands of people at a time, hoping they get someone to bite. And guess what? People click the links. If people weren't falling for it, you wouldn't keep getting these messages.

Criminals prey on fear and uncertainty, so they come with messages that claim to have things like the latest public health guidance. They even take advantage of people's good nature by roping them into donation scams. That's only the tip of the iceberg. Other common phishing attacks include:

- **Tech support scams:** This is when you're contacted by a hacker pretending to be from a company like Apple, Geek Squad, Dell, or any tech company. You might get a call, email, or text saying that you have a virus on your computer. They offer to help you get it off by directing you to a link that you click and then download software that gives them access to your computer. There are scam call centers that specialize in this particular scam, and most are not in the United States.

- **Shipping scams:** Have you ever gotten a message from someone pretending to be DHL, UPS, or FedEx claiming that you have a package? Well, those aren't real, and you don't want to click those links they send.
- **Impersonation Scams:** "$687.00 was withdrawn from your account at an ATM in Jacksonville, Florida. If this wasn't you, please click this link." There are different variations of these fraudulent loss-prevention calls, emails, or texts. Scammers will also pose as representatives from trusted institutions and agencies, such as the IRS. Just be aware that the IRS will never call you demanding money. The scammers behind this one are betting that you don't know that, which is why you might constantly receive these calls.
- **Quid pro quo attack:** This works by giving a favor for a favor. Scammers will contact you and offer a gift card or a free trial of some product if you try their software. They then send you a link to download that contains the malware needed to get your information.
- **Scareware:** These are the pop-up messages you get on your computer that say your computer has a virus and you need to install specific software to remove it, but all this does is download the actual malware to your device.

This list goes on and on to include tax scams, payroll scams, class action settlement scams, delivery failure notification scams, and faulty medical records transfers. There will probably be many, many more in the months to come.

Online scams are becoming more complex and involved, but we have noticed patterns that make it easier to predict potential targets. We will always have natural disaster scams. While the disaster may change, as long as people are trying to receive insurance money to fix their homes and repair their lives after a tragedy, some criminal organizations will try to systematically take advantage of that. The same is true when there is a significant government effort to distribute money. Whether COVID-19 relief or student loan forgiveness, any time there is a situation where people hope they might receive some monetary relief, that attracts scammers.

Veterans, active members of the military, and their families are another common target. In 2021, there was a 20 percent increase in incidents of identity theft, fraud, and digital crime among this group. The money lost to that fraud jumped a massive 118 percent from $122 million to $267 million during that same period.[12] That's an enormous disparity when compared to rate of identity theft among the average consumer. AARP research suggests they are being targeted by scammers who try to take advantage of military-related benefits and services.[13]

There are myriad ways criminals can steal from you, but just because you don't click suspicious links doesn't mean you're safe. Instead of casting a wide net and sending out phishing emails to thousands of people at the same time, more motivated hackers target individuals, through what is called spear phishing. That often requires conducting more background research of that one individual to effectively trick them into downloading links, or voluntarily giving up personal, financial, or company information and credentials.

Most every personalized cyberattack today has a technical side and a human side. It's this human side that has become the basis for what is known as social engineering attacks. While looking for digital weaknesses, these criminals also gain your trust by exploiting human nature to hack into your accounts. In 2021, cybercriminals used social engineering in 98 percent of attacks.[14]

With enough information, the scammer can target you directly. They can even spoof phone numbers and emails, so it looks like you are being contacted by a person or organization you trust. It might be a friend, colleague, coworker, or representative from a bank or financial institution. They then use false pretenses to trick you into divulging your personal, account, or login information.

One example is business email compromise where scammers can pose as other employees or trusted vendors to ask employees for information or request to change payroll or payments. They can also gain access to legitimate business emails, sometimes even an active thread, and use that to spread malware. Nobody realizes it's a threat because it's coming from inside the company. They try to be persuasive by creating a sense of urgency to get your guard down and your anxiety up, so you either volunteer your information or willingly download a link that contains malware. In 2021, the FBI received twenty thousand complaints of business email compromise, resulting in total losses of $2.4 billion.[15]

These types of social engineering attacks are exactly why many one-size-fits-all solutions fall short, and why we need more personalized protection.

## A Behind-the-Scenes Look at Phone Hacking

Let's go back and deconstruct what happened to Lauren, prior to her falling victim to the SIM swap when she woke up in the morning unable to access her phone.

Both Lauren and her husband were careful with their account numbers and passwords, but they weren't fully protected because so much of their personal data was online. With a simple Google search, the scammer could get her name, phone number, address, birthday, email address, and the name of her relatives. The information used to pull off this hack was most likely information Lauren gave away willingly that was then sold. That's enough to derail any authentication system that exists. And as we will discuss in the next chapter, the way data like this is bought and sold is completely legal right now.

With this basic information, the scammer called AT&T, pretending to be Lauren, and then transferred her account to T-Mobile and a SIM that he owned. That gave the scammer complete access to Lauren's phone while she was locked out. He could make phone calls, send texts, and access all of her apps. But how did he get access to the banking apps? Wouldn't he need a password? Yes, but since the scammer had access to her phone, he received the multifactor authentication code when he requested to change the password. He then reset her password, locked her out of her own account, and transferred all the money to a different account.

One of the most high-profile SIM swaps occurred in 2018 when cryptocurrency investor Michael Turpin lost $23.8 million in cryptocurrency. The heist was orchestrated by Ellis Pinsky, who was a fifteen-year-old high school student at the time.[16] Turpin went on to sue AT&T for $224 million, of which he was awarded $75.8 million.[17]

Wealthy individuals, particularly crypto investors, have become SIM swap targets because of how easy it is to quickly transfer funds, exchange them for different coins, and scatter them across numerous wallets. Given how lucrative these scams are, hackers recruit highly specialized and skilled freelancers to become part of a decentralized team that each play very specific roles throughout the scam.

A major part of this scam involves initiating the transfer with the mobile service provider. That can be done by posing as the victim, as in Lauren's case, but it isn't always that easy. Sometimes hackers must social engineer the manager to give up his credentials by impersonating the IT help desk when inquiring about a service ticket, and then sending the manager a link to a spoofed website asking for the manager's login. Sometimes they outright bribe the manager to give up their credentials or pay them to do the swap themselves. In some extreme cases, hackers will pay someone to simply snatch the tablet that managers carry with them throughout the store and bring it to the rest of the team who is typically waiting nearby to perform the SIM swap before the mobile company can disable and wipe the tablet. It's become big business and is nearly impossible to fend off an army of determined tech-savvy hackers, but SIM swaps aren't the only way hackers can gain access to your phone.

Just like with your computer, downloading phishing links from emails and text messages (also called smishing) are common ways scammers get you to download malware, so they can take over your phone. The same thing applies to apps. Don't be fooled by messages claiming to be legitimate companies you trust asking you to download an app, and don't be fooled by free games. They might be secretly installing software in the background. Never download apps from external sources, even if they look legitimate.

This type of malware sometimes comes in the form of scareware, or browser pop-ups that claim your device is infected. Scammers have found it highly effective to use your fear of being hacked against you. The pop-up directs you to download free apps they say will remove the malware from your phone when in reality, the app installs the malware. Just so you know, websites can't scan your phone and have no way of knowing if your device is infected, so these are always scams.

There is so much sensitive personal and financial information available on your phone that phone hacking has become the main target of many cybercriminal organizations. In 2020, forty-five thousand malicious apps were identified in various app stores, leading to an estimated 17.8 million phones infected with malware.[18] And don't assume that the Apple app store is an exception. That same year, twelve hundred malicious apps were available and downloaded more than 300 million times a month from the Apple app store.[19] Android devices and Google Play suffer from the same problems, so if you want to use a mobile device, there is no safe alternative.

If that doesn't work, hackers can also gain access to your phone through vulnerable Wi-Fi connections. Public Wi-Fi is especially susceptible to attack. Hackers can create malicious hotspots that appear legitimate. And once they have access to your phone, they can plant malware on your device to capture your personal and financial information. They can even learn the usernames and passwords to your various accounts.

It might not be a surprise that public Wi-Fi networks are relatively easy to hack, but did you realize the same is true about your home Wi-Fi network? Hackers can gain access to your phone and also your computer, tablet, or any device hooked up to that Wi-Fi. And I mean any device. In 2022 in the UK, a creepy hacker accessed a young couple's baby monitor to spy on and sometimes even talk to their two-year-old son.[20] That's enough to terrify any parent into thinking twice about which Internet of Things devices they bring into their homes.

People assume that since Wi-Fi routers don't store information, there is no need to protect them, but hackers can exploit outdated routers, firmware, and weak or default passwords to capture the sensitive data flowing through these devices. Your Wi-Fi router is just another vector of attack and potential vulnerability. This is why you always want to make sure your router is updated and you change the default password. It's a simple way to mask your digital footprint and further insulate your family.

There are multiple ways scammers can gain access to your phone, but ask any of them and they will tell you that it's always easier when victims willingly hand over access to their phones without realizing it. Scammers can install hardware into normal-looking public cell phone charging stations that allow them to infect a victim's device with malware or steal their data. The scam is called juice jacking, and it's incredibly successful because people will often use public charging stations without understanding or even thinking about the risk.

Just because your phone has been compromised, it doesn't mean that all hope is lost. Lauren didn't find out she was a victim of a SIM swap until it was too late, but there are other signs that your phone might have been hacked that you can look out for. Malware and malicious apps can drain your battery, use up data, and cause your phone to literally become hot. Look out for this unusual activity, along with frequent crashes and overall poor performance.

Even better than identifying the problem is preventing the attack from occurring in the first place. Later in the book, I'll go over simple steps you can take to lock your digital back doors and windows.

Lauren and her husband will spend the next few weeks dealing with the bank, but what happened to the hacker in this scenario? Does anybody go after him, or is there any way to track him down? Often in these cases, the stolen money is transferred to a recently opened account that is quickly emptied before anybody attempts to track it down. So, the simple answer is "no." Nothing happened to the scammer who cleaned out Lauren's family savings account.

## Why Cybercrime Is So Difficult to Prosecute

Cybercrimes aren't new crimes. What's new is the venue or the world in which they unfold. That's what makes it so appealing to criminal organizations. It allows them to make money in the shadows while taking minimal risk. It's simply a safer form of crime to commit because it can be conducted while remaining virtually anonymous.

Big data breaches make headlines. That's what gets the most attention and it's been the focus of recent legislation, but how many resources are state and local authorities allocating to investigate the people who steal *your* identity? It's those cybercriminals who prey on you and can wreak havoc on your life who are most likely to fly underneath the radar. Even if the authorities wanted to pursue these criminals, where would they start?

Cybercriminals have many tools at their disposal that help them wipe away their digital footprints and remain anonymous. They can work anywhere around the globe, making any investigation or arrest attempt a jurisdictional nightmare. It's difficult enough for law enforcement to get a handle on real-world crime. There has been progress, but the online world remains the equivalent of the Wild West, where everyone is forced to fend for themselves.

It will remain this way until the protection methods catch up to the sophistication of the crime committed online. But this is a losing battle if you're trying to fight it alone. These aren't lone actors you're up against; these are organized corporate ecosystems targeting you. It's entire teams of people working in foreign call centers and offices whose day jobs it is to steal your information and your money. They have the time, resources, and capability to search for vulnerabilities, exploit outdated solutions, and potentially attack you and your family in dozens of ways. On any given day, you might be open to a hundred different attacks. Nobody can guard against that. That's why you need a solution that doesn't only alert you of the problem but is three steps ahead of you, eliminating vulnerabilities and shutting down the potential avenues of attack.

I'm not trying to scare you. I'm trying to open your eyes to the risks and dangers you and your family face online, but I also want to make it crystal clear that you are not powerless.

You still play an active part in how your data is used on the internet. There are some fundamental protections and strategies you can immediately implement to take back control of your data and your safety. However, it will get worse before it improves, so you must be prepared. But how did it ever get to this point?

# CHAPTER 2

# The Information Economy Fueling the Fire

Have you ever been talking about something with a friend—a product, restaurant, anything at all—and then received an ad for that exact oddly specific thing on Instagram or Facebook? It's spooky. Almost like your phone is listening to your conversations. Well, your phone isn't listening (at least not yet), but it's doing many other things to keep tabs on you and your behavior. That's why when you search for a product, you're bombarded with more ads for similar products. It's why if you watch just one cat video on YouTube, hover over it even, you're doomed to a steady stream of cat videos from here on out. Welcome to the information economy! Enabling almost anything we desire to be only a click away has made life much more convenient, but it comes at a price, and that price is our privacy.

You might have heard the story about how Target learned a young woman was pregnant before her father knew and accidentally tipped him off through targeted advertising. The dad stormed into a Minneapolis Target, furious that they were sending his daughter coupons for baby clothes and cribs, only to learn after the fact that his high school daughter was, in fact, pregnant.

This anecdote is highlighted in a 2012 *New York Times* article[1] by Charles Duhigg, who explains how statisticians who worked for Target could determine which women were expecting based on their buying habits. The closer they looked, the more patterns they saw. For example, those women who switched to unscented lotions and soaps, purchased supplements such as zinc, calcium, and magnesium, or loaded up on hand sanitizer and washcloths, were more likely to be pregnant. Given the type of products purchased, they might even be able to determine the sex of the baby and when it was due. Target could then send those customers ads for products that might appeal to expecting mothers. And this story happened more than ten years ago. Imagine how sophisticated this technology is now.

Today, we're becoming more aware of how our data is used, and we understand that we're being targeted in ads, but most people have gotten used to it and grown to accept it. Many don't realize how vulnerable they are and don't completely understand the threat until it directly impacts their lives. That's when they start taking it seriously. But unfortunately, by that point, it's too late for many because the damage has been done, as seen in the case of those like Lauren. When looking at how we reached this point, it can all be traced back to data.

When we think of data, it's common to think of numbers scrolling down a green computer screen like in *The Matrix*, and in reality, that's not that far off. Computers constantly produce data, or metadata—which is data about data or, more specifically, categorizing data to understand the context and its relationship to other data.

To understand how this works, think about how you leave behind a trail when you venture out into the real world. Stop at a store; you're captured on video. Make a purchase with your credit card; there is a record of that transaction. Make a cell phone call; it pings a cell phone tower. While it's still possible to avoid detection when out and about, that is not a luxury you have when online or operating in the digital world. There is a record of almost every single thing you do online. All the devices you rely on daily create and store that data:

- **Your phone:** There is a record of everyone you call and text. Surf the internet, and there is a history of that as well. Unless you take steps to disable it, location services use GPS to track your movements and keep a record of where you go.

- **Your computer:** There is a record of every email you send and every online account you log into. You can go to incognito mode to search the internet, but that only prevents the browser on your computer from tracking you. Search engines and websites still compile information on your search history and the sites you visit when in incognito mode. When online shopping, not only is there a history of everything you purchase, but every page you visit is tracked.

- **Fitness trackers and watches:** These wearable devices can track your steps, heart rate, calorie intake, weight, and even your sleep patterns. That data is all uploaded online and stored, so there is a record.

- **Social media:** When you post something on Facebook, double tap what you like on Instagram, engage on TikTok or Snapchat, or talk and text on WhatsApp, you create more data.
- **Apps:** Yes, even the apps you download can collect your data and track your location. It's all laid out in the terms of service you most likely agreed to without reading.
- **Your car:** If your car has a factory-installed cellular connection, it's loaded with computers and cameras that calculate and monitor its function, performance, location, and even entertainment system. That data can alert you of problems and get you where you're going, but it's also collected and transferred back to the manufacturer.

This list could be expanded to include smart appliances connected to your phone through Wi-Fi and your home thermostat that tracks your energy usage. Even your pets can have chips in them to identify the owner. There is no escaping it.

Every single time you do anything online, you leave behind small pieces of your personal data, like bread crumbs. Sometimes that happens willingly, as when you publicly post information, and other times it happens without you even realizing that you're leaving anything behind. This data is immediately scooped up and stored. In his book *Data and Goliath*, author Bruce Schneier said that "data is the exhaust of the information age."

Because this data is becoming more valuable, the methods used to collect it are becoming more and more sophisticated. One of the most common ways this is done is through cookies. Most people have heard the term, but not everyone knows exactly what they are and how they work. Cookies are tiny files that are downloaded onto your device when you visit a website; they can be used to track your movements online, and they typically come in three forms:

- **Session cookies:** These are harmless and let you move from one part of a site to another without having to log in to every page, like when moving from a product page to a checkout page. These cookies are stored for the duration of the session and deleted after you leave the site.
- **Persistent cookies:** These can be a little more intrusive. These files remain on your computer to track your browsing history.
- **Third-party cookies:** These plant pieces of code on the browser to track your movements and are placed by companies other than the site you're visiting.

Java scripts and browser fingerprinting are more sophisticated methods that can be used with cookies to track your movements and have become more difficult for the user to avoid or disable. However, Google and Apple have started phasing out third-party cookies. That will change the digital landscape once again, but there is no doubt that marketing efforts will adapt. What we don't yet know are the unintended consequences that might emerge down the road, because there is no guarantee that new techniques will be safer or less invasive.

When compiled, all of this data reveals who you communicate with, where you go (how frequently and for how long), how much money you have, how much money you make, what you spend it on, news preferences, education level, marital status, homes you own, cars you've purchased, number of children you have, political affiliation, health information, personal and professional problems you might be experiencing, what you're concerned about, what you want to know more about, and where you are at this very moment. Even the typos and spelling errors you make in your Google searches can provide information. Your browser history alone can give tremendous insight into your thoughts, fears, desires, and dreams. Next time you're on your computer, click on the history tab and take a look at the story it tells. Spend enough time online, and your search history will reveal what you're thinking. It can be more revealing than a diary because you don't think to conceal or censor it, and that's just one of many data points.

Data is a blueprint for human behavior—who you are, how you think, and how you are likely to behave. That is very valuable information, and it is why companies go to such great lengths to acquire your data. But once they have it, what do they do with it?

## How Is Your Data Being Used?

There is no question that technology has made life incredibly convenient. Using the device in our pocket, we can look up any fact, find the answer to any question, read any book, watch any movie, and purchase almost any item and have it delivered to our door. We can communicate with practically anyone around the world, contact someone to pick us up and take us where we want to go, and not only receive detailed directions when driving but, based on real-time traffic, determine the fastest way to get there. Try convincing anyone thirty years ago that all of this would be possible in their lifetime.

What's even more amazing is that access to much of this entertainment, information, and services is free. However, there is a catch, and the reason why all this stuff is free is that you aren't the one consuming the product. *You are the product!* Many apps, services, retailers, and companies have realized that collecting data about their customers is more valuable than the products or services they sell. That gives them a strong incentive to sell that data to third parties, and it's become an indispensable second source of income for many companies. It's why they go to such great lengths to get that data. So, when companies want you to join loyalty programs in exchange for great deals on their products, you give them your data when you sign up, they give you a good deal, and then they turn around and sell that data. But who are they selling that data to?

This is where data brokers come in. You've probably heard the term before. You might have even heard of some of these companies: Acxiom, Epsilon, Oracle, Equifax, and Experian. Those are just some of the world's largest data brokers, but there are thousands that make up this secondary market of companies that have created a $200 billion-a-year industry. What they do is compile large sets of data from all those bread crumbs that you and millions of others have left behind when online. They not only buy their information in bulk from companies but also get it from government resources and credit bureaus. They then search for patterns and trends. They use all these little pieces of information to create a pro-file. They might find common connections, such as those who buy X also tend to buy Y. This is precisely how those at Target know when their customers might be pregnant and can adjust their advertising accordingly.

People are then sorted into endless categories. Wealthy singles, expecting parents, lonely seniors, and those suffering from debt are all potential categories data brokers can create. You can even be categorized by a medical condition. Diabetes, cancer, high blood pressure—all of this information can be ascertained by your browser history and other data points. The medical information you relay to your physician is highly protected under HIPAA, but the same regulation doesn't apply to your data, so what you search for and the bread crumbs you leave behind can be used to identify your medical conditions. Keep this in mind the next time you mindlessly type those symptoms into the WebMD search bar.

Once this data is sorted by data brokers, it's then sold to other businesses, primarily to marketing companies to push advertising on consumers who, based on their interests and buying habits, are most likely to buy what they're selling. This is spun as a service they provide the consumer by helping expose them to products they likely want to buy.

Companies like Google and Facebook are different because they don't sell your data to third parties since they run their own advertising platforms. They are so big and have so many users that not sharing your data gives them a competitive advantage, and the advertising they use it for is their primary source of income. So, if you use Google services—email, search engine, maps, etc.—the company compiles all that data, and instead of blanketing their customers with broad ads, they use that data to determine your preferences and send you targeted ads for products and services you're more likely to purchase based on recent behavior. Yes, they do use it to improve their services—so that's how you can learn the fastest route to your destination and receive a curated selection of videos on your YouTube feed—but it's primarily reserved for ads. That's their bread and butter. And your data is so valuable to them that they offer their services for free. If you want to keep using Google services, Instagram, and Facebook for free, it's impossible to prevent your data from being collected. That's the trade-off.

It's this practice that social psychologist and Harvard Professor Shoshana Zuboff dubbed "surveillance capitalism," and it was the subject of her 2018 book, *The Age of Surveillance Capitalism: The Fight for a Human Future at the New Frontier of Power*. Zuboff explains how Google pioneered this technology and transformed the old business model. She refers to them as the Ford Motor Company of surveillance capitalism. What began as a way to improve their search bar technology led them to learn about the power of ads based on behavioral predictions. Instead of viewing people as the product, Zuboff considers them the resources mined for these predictions that are sold to Google's advertisers. That proved to be so incredibly profitable that everyone tries to do it now.

Okay, it's easy to collect data, but so what? Who cares? What's the worst that can happen? If I'm not doing anything wrong, I have nothing to hide. Right? How is targeted advertising any worse than any of the old forms of advertising?

The problem is that advertisers are not the only group who can benefit and profit from your data. Nothing is stopping those third parties from turning around and selling that data to other groups and individuals with a completely different set of motives—motives that might not be entirely legal.

In order to shed light on the dark side of this industry, reporters have not only purchased data but they have also exposed some of the gray areas. Banks and insurance companies can use this data to determine your premium payments and if they want to give you a loan. Divorce lawyers and private investigators can use this data to build a case against you. Government agencies and law enforcement can bypass federal law by purchasing data without a warrant that they can then use to carry out criminal investigations and deportations. Authoritarian governments can use that data against their citizens to punish those who dissent.

Your data is being collected, stored, analyzed, bought, sold, and resold over and over again for millions and millions of dollars. It can also be hacked anywhere along the chain of sale. Yes, all these companies can also be hacked, the data brokers included, and that data can be sold on the dark web. And with the way technology is rapidly changing, this personal data now includes your genetic makeup. If you think your fitness tracker and the health app on your phone can provide remarkable data, that's nothing compared to what is going on in the world of genetics.

Whether curious about your family history or hoping to learn more about your own genetic makeup, there has been a boom in services that offer DNA analysis. GEDMatch is a personal genomics and genealogy website that has been used by many people, including adoptees looking to find their biological parents. It also serves as a shared database, so you can find family members or relatives who might have used other genealogy platforms, such as 23&Me or Ancestry.com. Dozens of websites offer these services, and the benefits go far beyond tracking down relatives. Discovering your genetic profile has tremendous health value, including learning about your susceptibility to certain conditions and diseases so you can take the necessary precautions. Knowing that you have a genetic predisposition to breast cancer or ovarian cancer can possibly save your life. However, we're just starting to learn the benefits of this data, and it's being used in unexpected ways.

In 2018, GEDMatch gained notoriety when it was used by law enforcement to identify and arrest Joseph James DeAngelo Jr., also known as the Golden State Killer. DeAngelo had committed more than fifty sexual assaults in Northern California during the 1970s before moving to Southern California, where he was believed to have committed twelve murders in the late 1970s and early 1980s. The FBI had the killer's DNA, and they routinely checked this with their own CODIS (Combined DNA Index System) database. However, this search was limited to parents, siblings, and children, so the investigation hit an impasse. That's when they got the idea to use the GEDMatch database because it had significantly more data that would allow them to find a link to more distant relatives. It was a shot in the dark, but it worked.

Investigators identified distant relatives of the killer. Based on what they knew about the killer, they narrowed down their list of suspects, and collected DNA samples from those suspects. It was DNA from a tissue taken out of a trash can that matched that of the killer they had on file and proved that Joseph James DeAngelo Jr. was the Golden State Killer. He was arrested and pleaded guilty to twenty-six charges, including thirteen counts of murder, and is now serving multiple life sentences. A serial killer who had eluded police for forty-four years was identified and apprehended in under six months using DNA technology. Suddenly, these DNA sites became a resource to help police solve cold cases where the killer's DNA was left at the scene. While this might sound like an excellent tool that could be used to solve murders and sexual assaults, this was completely uncharted territory, and authorities quickly found themselves in the legal gray area.

Since this type of massive DNA database was never accessible before, there weren't laws stipulating which information law enforcement could use and which they couldn't. During some of these investigations, even during the apprehension of the Golden State Killer, it was later revealed that these private for-profit companies violated their own privacy policies when handing over user data.[2] Some people didn't care and felt that this information should be accessible to law enforcement if it meant they could arrest killers and rapists while giving much-needed peace to the victims' families. But not everyone felt that way. Some saw the bigger picture and the possible trade-offs and consequences of publicizing this type of data, and they had good reason to worry.

Once again, many people don't view this as a problem, and they share the common theory that if they aren't doing anything wrong, they have nothing to hide. And part of that is true. Nothing might happen to many people who have made their genetic information available online, but we're only starting to venture into this uncharted territory. We don't yet know where this will go. While this genetic information is an excellent way to learn about what diseases and conditions you might be predisposed to, what if this information were to land in the lap of health insurance companies who could use it to raise your premiums, or worse, refuse to cover you because of those conditions? In this case, your data would be leveraged against you, and that's a trade-off that nobody wants to make.

Many of these genetic testing companies have changed their policies regarding data, and some have different policies about providing this data to law enforcement. Some companies only do so in extreme cases or to aid in the investigation of certain violent crimes. GEDMatch now allows users to opt out and not make their data available to law enforcement or not make it public at all. However, there is no consensus on what these companies can do with our data, which speaks to the bigger problem of data collection in the information economy.

What does the future hold? Instead of predicting behavior, could companies use this data to *engineer* behavior for the commercial needs of their advertisers? For instance, when you're driving, what if you get directions that take you on an alternate route, which happens to force you to drive by businesses you've been receiving targeted ads for? Surely, that's science fiction and taking things too far. There must be laws in place to prevent something that manipulative . . . right?

## How Is Any of This Legal?

One way data brokers defend their business model, and the entire practice of buying and selling data, is by claiming it's anonymous. So, if that data were to fall into the wrong hands, it couldn't be used against one individual. Or so they say.

While it's true that large swaths of this data commonly bought and sold may not directly identify individuals, it's not difficult to learn the identity of one of those individuals if you have their location data and can track their movements. This is precisely what CBS News tried to prove with a 2019 story on the business of location tracking data.[3]

Location data traditionally comes from the apps that track the movement of your phone. Some people know that you can turn this setting off, others don't, and some don't care. CBS News worked with a whistleblower whose job was to buy the location data of 80 million Americans, but after seeing how the company he worked for failed to prioritize the security of this data, he quit. Without letting on they were journalists, the reporters spent months contacting various data brokers before purchasing a large data sample that included the daily movements of fifteen hundred phones in the wealthy neighborhood of Greenwich, Connecticut. This data didn't have any names or phone numbers, but reporters could easily identify each user by where that person spent their nights. This data was so precise that it tracked some people more than two hundred times in a single hour.

This is all perfectly legal, but what if location data such as this were to get into the hands of a criminal organization? That could easily happen if one of these companies suffered a data breach and all that data was put up for sale on the dark web. That becomes a major security risk, but it's one that many people don't even recognize as a risk. One reason is that many people don't even know this is happening, at least not to this degree.

Most of us assume that we are in control of the data we put out into the world and that it's limited to the information we willingly give out, but that is far from the truth. If we were being tracked this way in the real world (like by a bad actor in a dark sedan), it would be disconcerting and seem excessive, but this type of digital surveillance was designed to go undetected. The entire point is that we don't know it's happening. But as long as we continue to live our lives online, essentially carrying a tracking device everywhere we go, that will be the reality.

What's scary is that this doesn't only put you at risk, it also puts your children at risk. In 1998, the Children's Online Privacy Protection Act (COPPA) was created to protect the privacy of children online, imposed by the Federal Trade Commission (FTC). While this requires parental consent for commercial websites to process the data of children under thirteen, it doesn't apply to nonprofits or the government. It also does not apply to data brokers.

There are few restrictions when it comes to advertising that targets kids. By the time a child is thirteen, online advertising firms have collected an average of 72 million data points about that child by tracking app activity.[4] What's more alarming is that even the few laws we have on the books aren't being enforced. Currently, one in five of the children's apps available on Google Play are in violation of COPPA rules. It was discovered that most of these apps that collect data don't differentiate between children and adults. And these are apps that have been downloaded by almost 492 million users, and many of them are labeled "teacher approved."[5]

But let's say you are concerned and want to do something about it; what can you do? What choice do you have? Are you and your family going to ban smartphone use? Never send an email or conduct a Google search ever again? You can choose not to participate in modern life, but how practical is that? We're in too deep to consider going totally off the grid. These devices and this technology have become a necessary component of how we all work and live, and it comes at the cost of our data and privacy. As long as you choose to participate in the modern world, your data is not your data anymore. In fact, if you want to take your data off the internet or don't want it to be used, you must go out of your way and sometimes even pay a company to do that for you. Think of how crazy it is that privacy is not the default option and that you must go out of your way to achieve it.

Because this problem didn't exist thirty years ago, there were no laws to protect us. Individual states have made strides to limit the way companies can use your data, but as of right now, there is no comprehensive federal privacy law. Some have been proposed, and minor regulations are in place, but nothing significant has yet been adopted. It doesn't help that both political parties in the United States successfully use this technology during their election campaigns to try and swing public opinion in their favor. And they've become very good at wielding this tool.

For the time being, we are at the mercy of the privacy policies of the companies whose products and services we use. These are policies that almost nobody reads, so we're agreeing to be willing participants without fully understanding what we're agreeing to. And this problem is only going to get worse. The declining cost of computing technology makes it easier and cheaper to gather and store more data, while technology changes the type of data that can be acquired and what can be done with that data. However, it's not all bad.

Yes, this data has been used to solve crime, improve medical treatments, and improve the quality of the products we purchase and services we're provided. As technology advances, we continue to find new ways that our data can be used, and there continue to be remarkable benefits, but we're starting to learn that for every possible benefit, there is usually a trade-off. The question becomes how much those trade-offs are putting you at risk and what you can actually lose.

# CHAPTER 3
# What's Really at Stake?

In 2019, a pregnant Teiranni Kidd checked into the Springhill Medical Center in Mobile, Alabama, prepared to give birth.[1] What she didn't know was that the center had recently suffered a ransomware attack. The center refused to pay the ransom, so its IT system was shut down for eight days, preventing staff access to equipment and medical records. During this eight-day window, Teiranni gave birth, but there were complications, and the umbilical cord was wrapped around her baby's neck. This resulted in brain damage that led to the baby's death nine months later. The machine that allowed nurses to detect fetal heartbeats could have alerted medical professionals to the situation beforehand, but doctors didn't have access to it. With more information and access to equipment, it's possible doctors would have tried to deliver the baby via cesarean section, thus preventing brain damage and saving the baby's life.

Unaware of the security breach before giving birth, Teiranni filed a lawsuit against the hospital, and a negligent homicide investigation followed. This was very murky, uncharted territory, so allegations varied about who was to blame, but what is clear is that a ransomware attack played a direct role in the loss of a life.

A similar incident occurred in Germany a year later when a patient who needed urgent care arrived at the Dusseldorf University Hospital only to be turned away because it had been shut down after a similar ransomware attack. This patient was taken to another hospital twenty miles away, but the hour-long delay proved fatal, and she passed away before being properly treated.

These types of ransomware attacks on hospitals and health care facilities grew more common during the COVID-19 pandemic, and a 2021 Ponemon Institute Report concluded that these attacks significantly impacted patient safety, data security, and overall patient care. Forty-three percent of the six hundred IT and healthcare security professionals surveyed said their organizations experienced a ransomware attack, and 45 percent of those feel those attacks disrupted and hindered the level of care their facilities could provide.[2,3] It led to extended patient stays and delays in testing. If this trend continues, they believe it can lead to an increase in both patient complications and mortality rates.

Some cybercriminals and organizations have no qualms about putting human lives at risk, which makes these attacks more dangerous than ever. And it's not just hospitals that are targeted.

All different sectors of the economy can be affected. On May 7, 2021, the Colonial Pipeline in Houston, Texas, which supplied gasoline and jet fuel to 45 percent of the East Coast, suffered a ransomware attack that halted operations and compromised data. A state of emergency was declared for seventeen states and Washington, DC, until the pipeline could resume normal operations on May 12.

In 2022, a group of hackers called Vice Society unleashed a ransomware attack on the Los Angeles Unified School

District (the second-largest district in the United States) that disrupted the system of more than one thousand schools, impacting more than six hundred thousand students. When the ransom wasn't met, the group exposed enormous amounts of data that included personal, health, and financial information of students and employees.[4] Attacks like these are not only disruptive, but they can cause tremendous damage. According to a study by Comparitech, in 2021, sixty-seven ransomware attacks affected 954 schools and colleges, possibly impacting 950,129 students and potentially costing the institutions a combined $3.56 billion in downtime.[5] That doesn't even take into effect the impact it can have on student learning.

These high-profile ransomware attacks are becoming more common, and it's not only governments and businesses that are impacted; they are dangerous for everyday families. Many of the victims in these types of attacks are not the direct target, yet the impact on their lives can be devastating.

All of these examples have been reported on and made the news because of the disruption they caused and the damage done. What you don't hear as much about are the attacks on consumers. Those stories may not make for great headlines, but they are much more common, and can be equally devastating for those targeted. If cybercriminals can shut down hospitals, disrupt utility services, create school closures, and block access to government resources, all of which require hacking more robust digital security systems, imagine the damage that can be inflicted on you and your family. Without the proper digital protections in place, you are an easy target.

According to the Federal Trade Commission, 5.7 million Americans were victims of identity theft and fraud in 2021, making it the worst year in history for that type of crime.[6] It's safe to say that identity theft is quickly becoming the crime of the century, but what exactly does that mean, and how can you be impacted?

When discussing cybercrime, identity theft, and hacking, financial fraud is the first thing people think of—and with good reason, because it can be devastating. Your savings accounts can be drained, and your credit cards maxed out. The cumulative losses of American victims of identity theft are in the billions each year, and that's terrifying, but it's not just money you can lose.

Your credit score is one of your most valuable financial assets and, if not properly safeguarded, one of your most vulnerable. Payment history, credit use, and length of credit history all determine your credit score, and if thieves gain control of your credit card numbers, they can run up massive bills and do a tremendous amount of damage in a short period. Missing just one payment on a credit card you didn't even realize existed in your name could drop your score one hundred points. Even if the credit companies can detect the fraud and you aren't on the hook for the bill, repairing the damage done to your credit score is a different hassle altogether. It can even prevent you from qualifying for mortgages, loans, and even certain jobs. Or, in my case, having to file taxes in person to prove I am who I say I am.

This can happen slowly, but those who don't regularly check their credit won't notice their score begin to tick downward. Monitoring your credit can also make you aware of any hard inquiries. Unlike the soft inquiries made by your bank or any companies looking to preapprove you, a hard inquiry is a sign that someone else is using your name to apply for credit. Unfortunately for many, the first sign that their credit score has been impacted occurs when they receive calls from collection agencies or apply for a new line of credit and are denied.

All that personal data flying around the internet leaves you exposed to a host of issues that can impact you and your family in a way that you might not suspect. Do you have any embarrassing or compromising information or pictures on your devices? Have you sent any incriminating emails? Cybercriminals can post that information, or worse, blackmail you into forking over a hefty sum of money to keep them from posting it. This can ruin your reputation, and sometimes that's much harder to repair than your credit score.

Even if you manage to recover from one incident relatively unscathed, these attacks often aren't only a one-time occurrence, and it doesn't mean you are no longer a target. If anything, the opposite is true. Once your identity is stolen, you're at a higher risk of it happening again. You can always change your usernames, passwords, email addresses, and phone numbers. You can't as easily change your name and Social Security number. With some information, once it's out there, it's out there. The ITRC reported that 30 percent of identity theft victims are people who have already had their identity stolen. Twenty percent of those repeat victims lost more than $21,000 across multiple attacks.[7] With data breaches increasing 68 percent from 2020 to 2021,[8] there is no reason to think cybercrime will slow down. That means each year more and more of your data will be exposed, but what impact can that have on you?

While it may be difficult to trace any individual cyberattack back to a specific data breach, evidence shows that having your information leaked in a breach increases the likelihood that you will fall victim to an attack. A 2021 F-Secure survey referred to those who have had their data leaked as "The Walking Breached," and 60 percent of that group experienced one or more types of cybercrime in one year compared to only 22 percent of those whose data wasn't leaked in a breach.[9]

This trend is even more pronounced among parents. A family with one or more children has a larger digital footprint than a single individual or a couple without children. It makes sense because they have more devices to secure and thus more potential vulnerabilities. That's why 70 percent of parents whose information was leaked in a breach experienced one or more types of cybercrime in a year compared to only 48 percent of individuals without children whose data was breached.[10]

We're also starting to see scary examples of how information leaked in a data breach can have dangerous real-world consequences. When the crypto wallet company Ledger was hacked in 2020, the names, emails, and physical addresses of 270,000 customers were leaked. These individuals reported phishing and SIM-swapping attacks, but some were even threatened with physical attacks. Since criminals had the home address of these customers, some received threatening messages demanding payments or risk home invasion if they didn't hand over their crypto wallet.[11]

That takes the nature of the threat posed by data breaches to a new level, but the story doesn't end there. In the wake of the breach, some victims received a package with a letter on company stationery, complete with a replacement Ledger device, only to learn after the fact that it was a scam. Those who installed those devices put all of their cryptocurrency at risk. This was something many people, even Ledger, didn't see coming.[12] And it's just another example of how attacks continue to evolve and grow more sophisticated.

Many responsible people don't take this threat as seriously as they need to because they don't think they are at risk. They assume that the careless, the misinformed, or the unsuspecting elderly are the most vulnerable, while they themselves are careful, fully informed, and effectively suspicious. It's easy to assume that high-profile people and the most uber-wealthy are the ones who are targeted through personalized attacks. *With so many bigger fish out there, who would come after me?* And while all of that might be true, it's only partially true. Those previously mentioned individuals might be more high-profile targets of cyberattacks, but that doesn't make you or the average family less susceptible. One characteristic of modern cybercrime is that it doesn't discriminate. Let's take a closer look at the actual stats.

## Who Are the Most at Risk?

Much depends on the individual, their online habits and behaviors, and the level of protections they have in place, but there are some trends worth noting. According to the *Gen-Z Fraud Report: Young Americans & Fraud*, here is the breakdown for average losses per victim by age:[13]

- Under 20: $3,061
- Age 20–29: $2,789
- Age 30–39: $5,570
- Age 40–49: $7,832
- Age 50–59: $9,864
- Age 60+: $9,174

These stats can be somewhat deceiving. Many older Americans tend to be less technologically savvy and have more money than younger people, so they make much better targets, and it's no surprise that the average loss per victim is higher in those age brackets. However, just because young people grew up around technology doesn't make them immune to cybercrime.

They might not have as much money to lose, but those aged eighteen to twenty-nine are more likely to become victims of identity theft for the simple reason that they are digital natives. Since they grew up with this technology, it's ingrained in their lives. They can easily become a little too comfortable with social media, and are more likely to share their personal information, only because it's all they know.

Truecaller Insights looked at cybercrime by gender in their "2022 U.S. Spam and Scam Report,"[14] and found that men were more likely to be victims of scams than women, particularly younger men. Forty-six percent of men aged eighteen to thirty-four lost money due to phone scams, compared to only 24 percent of men aged forty-five to fifty-four. A big driver of this in recent years has been romance scams on various dating sites.

The reality is that fraud can strike at any time and often in unexpected ways, which makes it difficult to predict and protect against. And no two cases are the same because there are so many variables and circumstances to consider. Since not all identity theft and cybercrime result from being careless online, it's even more challenging to predict and defend against.

Cybercrime can often originate with a crime in the real world. A stolen wallet, purse, or phone can give cybercriminals more information than they could ever dream of digging up online. It's like throwing open the door of your digital vault and leaving it wide open for scammers to ransack. In these cases, it doesn't matter how careful you are with your information online.

With only your license, criminals instantly have access to your full name, date of birth, address, driver's license number, signature, picture, and physical characteristics. This is why you want to leave your Social Security card at home and only carry those credit cards you need because you want to avoid giving criminals any more personal information. Having your driver's license confiscated is bad enough but add your phone to the mix of stolen property, and the severity of the problem escalates exponentially. Just ask James Bell.

In June 2022, James left the pub and was heading down a quiet residential street on the way back to his London home when he was mugged by four men. They took his wallet and phone, but they didn't stop there. They threatened him further if he didn't hand over his account PINs and use Face ID to unlock his banking app.[15] Luckily, he wasn't hurt further, and the thieves let him go, but by the time he phoned the police, his bank account was empty, and he couldn't get into his email or other accounts. Essentially, he was locked out of his life.

This is an extreme case, and you don't need to be violently mugged to have your phone stolen. Many people are careless with their phones when out in public, and thieves can easily swipe them from unsuspecting victims. One simple way to protect your information is to make sure the auto-lock is turned on. It doesn't make your phone unhackable, but it does give you a fighting chance. When losing your phone, the best-case scenario is that you have to purchase a new one. It stinks, but that's much less costly and less of a headache than thieves having access to that treasure trove of personal and financial information. Between bank accounts, credit card numbers, emails, photos, videos, and contacts, the sky is the limit as to the damage that can be done with that information.

Some safeguards are in place when your information and accounts have been compromised, so all hope is not lost, but that doesn't always make repairing the damage easy or fast.

## How Long Does It Take to Recover from Fraud?

Remember Lauren? The one who fell victim to the SIM swap? Her nightmare didn't end when she learned that $80,000 had been stolen from her bank account. It was only getting started.

Lauren didn't have a landline, so she had to borrow her husband's phone. Her first call was to the bank, but after an hour and a series of transfers, she couldn't speak with anyone who understood what was happening, never mind someone who could help get her money back. Her next call was to the police to file a report. After hanging up, she and her husband spent the rest of the day trying to change all their usernames and passwords, only to learn Lauren was also locked out of her Gmail. That meant she couldn't access her Google Drive, which was essential for her job since she started working from home.

The following day, Lauren went into her local bank branch in person and was able to speak with someone in the legal department. He started to make calls, but even though he worked for the bank, he was given the same unhelpful answers and encountered the same roadblocks she had the day before. They agreed to open an investigation, but she left the bank feeling completely helpless.

After ten days, and no updates from the bank or the police, she turned to a local detective. He proved more helpful. He did some digging, and learned that the fraud was set in motion when the thief walked into an AT&T store in New Jersey and added his name to her cellular account. The thief then transferred that number to another phone and performed the SIM swap that resulted in the hijacking of her accounts. This was reported to the police, but they had no way of identifying the suspect. The detective was also able to work with the bank to determine that Lauren's money was transferred to a different bank but arrived at a dead end because the two banks wouldn't communicate with each other.

It was a mess. The bank, the police, and the phone company all had different pieces of the puzzle, but getting them to work together, or even speak with each other, seemed impossible. What felt like the final nail in the coffin occurred six months after the initial incident when she received a letter from her bank in the mail informing her that they were closing the investigation. The bank couldn't prove foul play, and she would not be getting her money back. To add insult to injury, she could never regain access to her Gmail account and had to create a brand-new one.

Outside the financial loss, the most significant damage was psychological. She saw digital red flags everywhere and became paranoid that the slightest hiccup could be a sign of fraud. She hasn't given up hope yet and is pursuing alternative avenues to get her money back but has finally accepted that she might not be reimbursed.

We're often asked how long it takes to recover from fraud, but every situation and case of fraud or identity theft is different, so there is no simple, one-size fits all answer. It really comes down to three main factors:

## #1. What Type of Fraud Occurred?

The simpler the fraud, the simpler the resolution, which means the most basic types of cybercrime can be resolved quickly. A hacker locking you out of your Instagram account is a minor annoyance that could be straightened out in a few hours. A transaction on your credit card that you didn't make might only require a quick phone call to straighten out. That's good news, but it's the best-case scenario. If your information is acquired during a data breach and then sold on the dark web to organized cybercriminals who use it to hack into your accounts and run up your credit, what follows could be a nightmare.

Equally important as the type of fraud is which information was used to commit the fraud. As mentioned, you can change your credit card numbers, but changing your Social Security number isn't so easy, so if a criminal uses that to claim a tax refund from the IRS, it might take months to resolve. The same is true about medical identity theft. Dealing with the insurance company can be a time-consuming process. If a criminal cloned your identity and used your data to create fake driver's licenses, passports, or new credit accounts, that's an even more complicated problem that could drag on for months.

You can't possibly monitor all public records to see if your identity has been used during a crime, but it's that type of monitoring that can result in early detection, which is the second factor in determining the extent of the damage.

## #2. How Quickly Did You Discover the Fraud?

The longer a criminal can use your identity and access your accounts, the more damage can be done. That's why detection is so important, and it's what makes that fraud alert notification that many of these services provide so valuable.

If you can detect unusual spending habits first, you can resolve a problem quicker than if it lingers until you're locked out of your account, or your card is denied. And definitely before you start receiving notices from government agencies about tax returns you didn't submit or hear from creditors looking to collect on purchases you didn't make. Unfortunately, this is how most Americans learn they have become a victim of identity theft, and the damage is already done by that point.[16]

It's so important to keep an eye out for warning signs. This sounds so simple, and it really is . . . at first. But it's a lot to keep track of because there are so many different attack vectors. Here are just a few of the most common warning signs:

- **Financial accounts:** If you can't sign into your online accounts or notice strange charges to your bank account or credit card statement, you might have been a victim of account takeover. Luckily, some credit card companies and banks will reach out with a text or email to verify a large or unusual purchase, or one from out of state. This is a warning sign of possible identity theft that you shouldn't ignore. Another warning sign is a text with multifactor authentication verification codes from your accounts when you didn't ask for it. This could mean that someone is attempting to hack into your account.

- **Credit:** If scammers open up other financial accounts in your name, you won't be notified by mail, but if they run up additional lines of credit you didn't sign up for, that will impact your credit score. Most people don't keep tabs on their credit score, but simply checking it regularly can help you identify sudden dips that might be an early indication of identity theft or fraud. If you miss this, the damage can escalate, and then you might be denied credit when you legitimately apply (like me), or worse, start receiving calls from debt collectors for debt you didn't accrue.

- **Email and social media accounts:** The most common warning sign of email or social media account takeover is an inability to sign into your accounts. The second is when your contacts inform you that they've received strange messages from your accounts that you didn't send. These often come in the form of phishing links scammers send to your contacts.

- **Medical information:** Be on the lookout for incorrect information on your medical records or bills for procedures and prescriptions you never received. If your legitimate claims are denied by your insurance because you've used up your benefits or they claim preexisting conditions you don't have, immediately contact your medical provider and insurance company.

- **Unemployment benefits:** If your legitimate unemployment claims are denied, you receive a 1099-G tax form with the wrong information or unexpected paperwork from your employer or the government explaining unemployment benefits you never filed, you're most likely a victim of unemployment theft.

- **Tax information:** If you try to file your taxes and receive a notification from the IRS that someone has already filed taxes in your name, if there are records with the IRS or Social Security Administration from a job you never had, or you have been assigned an Employee Identification Number (EIN) you never applied for, immediately contact those agencies.

- **Title and home:** If you own a second home and start receiving utility bills from a vacant house, unfamiliar bills in your name, or stop receiving bills that you're used to getting, those can all be warning signs of potential deed fraud, as are mortgage notices and foreclosure notices for a home you don't own.

Luckily, some government and financial institutions have protections and fraud alerts to notify you of this unusual activity. These can help tip you off to potential fraud, so don't ignore any email, text, letter, or phone call from a lending company, account provider, or government agency. But these don't catch everything; some scams can bypass these alerts.

However—and this is a big "however"—it's important not to confuse any correspondence from your financial institutions with popular phishing scams that ask you to click links, send money, or send account information. The only information you should provide are "yes" or "no" responses to the inquiry. Never give out your name, account number, password, or any financial information over the phone. When in doubt, call the institution and confirm that a hold or alert has been placed on your account. And don't assume that these fraudulent charges to your account will always be big purchases. Sometimes, scammers begin with small test purchases to make sure the credit card or account they are charging is still active and see if it will go unnoticed. So, don't ever let any unauthorized transaction slide, no matter how small.

I'm sure reading all that is exhausting—keeping track of it is even more difficult, especially considering what might be happening with your kids and aging parents. Keeping your family safe online can become a full-time job, and it's not practical to assume you'll be able to identify all these warning signs immediately when they occur.

Many of these warnings have become white noise. Almost every day, there is news of a data breach. We receive constant alerts and notifications that our information may be at risk. Even robocalls and scam text messages are so common that we've given up trying to stop them and have learned to ignore them. We instinctively let our guard down, so we can easily miss something that, in hindsight, seems so obvious.

Knowing what to look out for is half the battle, but given our busy lives, it's easy for red flags to go unnoticed, thus creating a much bigger problem that can take much longer to recover from. That's when the third variable comes into consideration.

## #3. How Much Time and Money Are You Willing to Spend?

Recovering from fraud can be time-consuming and expensive, especially if crucial information was used and the crime wasn't identified early.

Few people know how much time and money it takes to recover from cybercrime better than Dave Crouse.[17] When he first noticed the usual charges on his statement in 2009, he immediately contacted his bank and opened a new account with a different bank. However, the worst was yet to come because he didn't realize scammers had opened their own accounts with his information. They spent $987,000 before they were apprehended. Crouse's life was turned upside down, and his career ruined. Not only was his savings account bled dry, but he spent $100,000 of his own money repairing the damage.

In many cases, the burden falls on the victim to sort everything out. And most people who fall victim to fraud, scams, or identity theft find themselves in entirely new territory. It's confusing and overwhelming. Sometimes it's difficult to wrap your head around what's actually happened. Not everyone knows exactly what they need to do because they've never experienced anything like this before. That means they might make mistakes and not take all the necessary steps to stop the bleeding and insulate themselves from future attacks. For example, if you've suffered from identity theft or an account takeover, as Lauren did in the first chapter, these are the steps you immediately want to follow:

1. Call the company where the fraud has occurred to alert them of the problem. Freeze your accounts and get new cards. You want to do this whether someone hacked into your existing account, opened another account, or made fraudulent charges in your name.

2. Ask these financial companies to send you a letter acknowledging that you are not liable for the

fraudulent charges and that they have been removed from your credit report.

3. Place a fraud alert with any of the three credit bureaus. You typically have three options:

   a. **Security freeze:** This prevents your report from being shared with third parties until it's lifted and is a good option if you are the victim of identity theft.

   b. **Initial fraud alert:** This requires lenders to verify your identity before approving new credit. It lasts for one year, but you can choose to lift it sooner.

   c. **Extended fraud alert:** If you remain at risk for fraud or identity theft, you can extend this alert for up to seven years. At any time, you can remove these freezes free of charge.

4. Freeze your credit. This prevents anyone else from accessing your credit report or opening a line of credit in your name. If you go this route, you must contact all three bureaus and then contact them again when you need a new line of credit.

5. Request a free credit report and scan it for anything suspicious.

6. Once you know the scope of the damage, file an identity theft report with the FTC (Federal Trade Commission). They will provide a plan and make an official record in case of any dispute.

7. File a claim with local law enforcement. Ask for the fraud department and have your FTC identity theft report ready.

Every step of the way, you always want to ask for documents relating to the fraud because it can help you dispute the charges when filing an identity theft report. It may sound excessive, but this is all standard procedure. Under the Fair Credit Reporting Act (FCRA), you have the right to dispute inaccurate information on your credit report.

This process is similar for each type of fraud and identity theft. For example, if your license is stolen, you want to contact the DMV to replace it and ask them to place a "Verify ID" flag on your license because this will alert law enforcement that your license has been stolen if anyone else tries to use it. It wouldn't hurt to request a copy of your driving record to see if any tickets had been issued in your name, or if there are any outstanding violations. If you believe the license was stolen, file a police report. You can go a few steps further and check with the United States Postal Service to make sure nobody has filed a change of address and run a background check.

When it comes to a lost or stolen phone, you first want to determine if it was, in fact, stolen. It's twice as likely that your phone is simply lost,[18] but if it does get stolen, the first thing you want to do is lock your phone remotely. This can be done by logging into your iCloud with your Apple ID on another device and enabling the Find My iPhone feature. The same process can be done on an Android by logging into your Google account, enabling the Find My Device feature, and selecting "Secure Device." You want to change your passwords to any vulnerable accounts or apps on your phone and enable multifactor authentication. Cancel any credit cards linked to Apple or Google Pay. Immediately report the theft to your mobile provider and block your SIM to stop scammers from using your phone. You might as well consider your phone gone, but you still want to erase your data remotely using the "Find My" app and file a police report.

Yes, it's a lot, and it's overwhelming. Having to do all this is not ideal, and so many people get so beaten down by this process that they eventually tap out. And even once the issue is resolved, in some cases, you will still have to prove that you are you. This is one of the reasons why I started Aura. However, we've yet to touch on one of the most debilitating effects that can occur when you become a victim of fraud.

## The Emotional Toll

We've talked a lot about the loss of money and time, but it's difficult to quantify what this experience does to your psyche, especially when your kids are involved, or your family is at risk. This process can be frustrating, stressful, and also embarrassing. Identity theft, fraud, and scams are just as much emotional crimes as they are financial.

One reason I use composite examples in the book is that many of the people victimized by these scams feel ashamed and violated. They don't want to come forward and share their stories. That's understandable because when you've had your most personal information exposed, you can't help but feel used and vulnerable. Even if you haven't lost much money and can quickly recover, it's still an awful feeling. That's why the Department of Justice estimates that only 15 percent of fraud victims report the crime.[19]

It doesn't matter how common these stories are and how easy it is for responsible people to fall victim to identity theft; there is no getting around the toll this experience takes on your mental health. The Identity Theft Resource Center (ITRC) learned that 77 percent of participants reported increased stress, and 55 percent experienced increased fatigue and decreased energy.[20] What nobody has been able to study yet are the long-term effects, specifically trust issues that develop over time.

It doesn't have to be this way, and that's where intelligent safety comes in. While there are a lot of great solutions to protect different vulnerabilities, there isn't one solution to protect you from all those vulnerabilities, until now. Having been a victim myself, I can understand and appreciate how damaging cybercrime can be to the average family who, because they don't realize they are vulnerable, don't have the proper protections in place. Intelligent safety is a technological solution that can handle all of this for you and do something even better: it watches your back and proactively prevents these issues from ever occurring in the first place. That can give you peace of mind and free up your time, so you can focus on what's most important to you and your family. What follows is our vision and an explanation of how it works.

# CHAPTER 4
# The Data Privacy Movement

In December 2013, smack in the middle of the holiday shopping season, Target learned their systems had been hacked. When they looked into the issue, they discovered it was much worse than expected. The information of 70 million customers, including 40 million credit card and debit card numbers, had been leaked online.

It was the largest retail data breach in US history at the time, and the fallout was devastating. Sales and profits drastically dropped. Lawsuits were filed, and the fines, settlements, and costs associated with recovering from the breach were estimated to be more than $200 million.[1] Target replaced its chief information officer (CIO), responsible for the security of their technology systems, and later fired its CEO.

A lengthy investigation revealed that Target was compliant with existing digital safety regulations and fulfilled their necessary requirements only months before the breach occurred. They had the best software and hundreds of IT professionals, which made them far more protected than most organizations, yet they weren't secure.

It turned out that the hack wasn't the fault of Target's employees or their lack of security, at least not entirely. It occurred when an employee of the HVAC company hired by Target opened a phishing link containing the malware. Target's systems had the software to prevent that malware attack, but the third-party vendor they hired did not. The hackers then used the third party's login credentials to access Target's system and released a different attack. There was nothing special about that malware. It was not particularly sophisticated and probably cost a couple thousand dollars on the dark web, but it almost caused the destruction of a major corporation.

The Target hack was only the beginning. Much bigger data breaches have occurred since, and they are so common that it's become difficult to keep track. When news breaks of a breach, the initial reaction is to punish the company, but should a company's IT department be held directly responsible? Investigations revealed that some warning signs and alerts went unseen by Target IT professionals. They had turned certain security features off, opting instead for a manual overview, but most significant data breaches aren't the result of negligence. It's not that simple.

In the world we live in today, data breaches are unavoidable. Most companies that suffer breaches aren't careless with their customers' data and try to follow best practices. Many breaches occur when hackers exploit short-term vulnerabilities in their systems that haven't been patched up or updated.

Hackers are constantly searching for vulnerabilities and only have to be right once. It might take 10,000 attempts, and those first 9,999 are thwarted, but nobody ever hears about a breach that *didn't* happen. They only hear about the breach that *did*. That's the story that makes headlines, not everything the company might have done to insulate itself from further damage or prevent other attacks altogether. What everyone hears about is essentially an anomaly. A one in ten thousand moonshot.

Try thinking of it this way: Picture a ten-story office building. Now picture all of the piping that zigzags between the floors and walls of that building. There are miles of piping that extend in all directions. Some weaknesses in that piping can be detected, and problems can be avoided, but no building maintenance crew can be expected to prevent every problem. Even the most high-tech and well-maintained equipment will break or leak at some point-in-time. Nobody in that building can do anything to prevent that. They are limited by the equipment available to them. A company's digital security system operates in much the same way. The protections extend out in every direction, but no matter how well tended the system is, at some point, it will spring a leak. If just one minor vulnerability is exposed for only a brief period, all of the company's data can be exposed.

Even the most vigilant companies can't be expected to patch every vulnerability in real time, just like a building's maintenance staff can't be expected to prevent every single leak. The primary goal should not be to prevent the breach from happening. That's a losing battle for anyone choosing to fight it in the information economy. Because the problem has many layers of complexity, there is no easy solution, but the first step is to go after the source, and the source of the problem is the way data is collected and distributed. Specifically, it begins with regulation.

## What Does the Law Say?

The landmark General Data Protection Regulation (GDPR) went into effect in 2018 and is the European Union's attempt to address this growing problem. This law gives European citizens control over how organizations process and collect consumer data while doling out penalties to those who don't comply with the guidelines. When a breach occurs, companies must inform all affected within seventy-two hours. This one set of guidelines applies to all twenty-seven countries in the European Union.

Under GDPR, six lawful bases allow companies to process an individual's data.

1. Individuals provide consent.
2. Performance of a contract.
3. Legitimate interest.
4. Protect a vital interest.
5. Legal requirements.
6. Public interest.

When data is collected, companies must inform individuals what data they will collect, how they plan to use it, and who they will share it with. Users have the right to see, export, and delete their data. This means every citizen in the European Union has the right to have their data deleted; the right to be forgotten. That's a right that most citizens of the United States don't have, with the exception of California, which has its own data privacy law, the California Consumer Privacy Act (CCPA).

Right now, we in the United States have very few rights regarding our data. Most of the laws that govern the internet and data privacy were made decades ago, when the internet looked very different than it does now. That is a significant concern, given the data we produce and the data companies manage and use is growing exponentially. With every online account we set up, each online shopping transaction we make, and social media post we engage with, our future exposure increases. Our data contains our most intimate, identifiable, and valuable details, from health information to financial transactions, and even our very identity. We should have the right to prevent that data from being collected without our consent. We should have the right not to have that data collected and sold to data brokers. We should have the right to make sure our data is not used against us or to manipulate us because today, data rights are human rights.

Since GDPR went into effect across Europe, we've seen what's worked well and what hasn't. For one, companies have received fines when they didn't report breaches immediately. And many major corporations have been fined for not adhering to regulations. Marriott was hit with the equivalent of a $23 million fine, British Airways $26 million, H&M $41 million, Google LLC $68 million, Facebook $68 million, WhatsApp $255 million, and Amazon was hit with a whopping $877 million fine.[2] That's a ton of money, but many feel it isn't enough because the profits generated from these practices still outweigh the fines imposed for breaking the law.

An even bigger concern centers around the idea of consent. While users can view, download, and delete their data, companies have found ways around the rule of receiving consent from individuals before collecting their data. Sometimes companies are vague in their definition of what is considered a "legitimate interest." Sometimes you must accept the website's cookie policy in order to read the cookie policy. And other times, instead of asking users to opt into the tracking, they are automatically enrolled and given the option to "opt out," but the process of opting out is so complicated that people don't want to be bothered. That happens when those collecting the data are the same ones drawing up the consent form and profiting from it.

Something else we've learned since the implementation of GDPR is that if given a choice, most people will choose convenience over privacy. That doesn't mean that they don't want privacy. It means that they aren't willing to sacrifice convenience for it. Even when told how their data is being collected and used, they still opt in. So, even with these regulations, very little has changed regarding online privacy.

Regardless of these drawbacks, GDPR is still a good first step. At least consumers are more aware that their data is being collected and how their privacy is being compromised. And the actions of corporations are being governed by laws developed in this century. Federal laws in the United States are almost two decades old, and there is nothing in those doctrines that prevents our data from being abused. Five states have established their own guidelines; the most stringent is California's implementation of the CCPA, which went into effect in 2020. Its scope is not as broad as GDPR, but it's a move in the right direction. Colorado, Connecticut, Utah, and Virginia are the other states that have implemented legislation, and some state's laws are stricter than others, but what this patchwork creates more than anything is confusion.

Most of the recent talk in political circles has been focused on the online safety of children. We're learning how technology can be addictive and how kids are targeted in unhealthy ways through apps and online games that incentivize them to keep playing. In response to high-profile criticism of these trends, a shift has occurred to give parents more control over the content their children consume.

The Children's Online Privacy Protection Act (COPPA), established in 1998 to protect the processing data of children under thirteen, has been a springboard for future legislation. There has been a move to amend COPPA and raise the age limit for protections to include those under eighteen. New bills have been proposed to further protect children from targeted advertising. Kids need to learn how to remain safe online, and parents need to play a role in protecting their children's personal information, but families shouldn't have to bear the entire responsibility. A healthier environment should be created to support these families.

The ideal solution would be a federal effort to simplify and unify these regulations. There is a move in Congress gaining momentum to create legislation, and we're starting to see collaboration on both sides of the aisle. Almost everyone agrees that there needs to be more transparency, so customers know what data is being collected, how it's being used, and can opt out if they want, but we're still far away from seeing something with any teeth get passed.

Part of the problem is the complexity of the subject matter. Most lawmakers aren't digitally savvy. Their lack of knowledge on the subject is displayed every time they question tech industry leaders. When Mark Zuckerberg testified before Congress, it was clear that many lawmakers didn't understand his platform, how it worked, or its profit model. That's changing. It's fair to say that lawmakers are becoming more knowledgeable as digital safety becomes a bigger issue, and they witness how much harm can be done online. However, with such rapid innovation, and the creation of new online spaces we can't easily monitor or even see, any law crafted could quickly become obsolete.

I can envision an effort from associations, nonprofits, and maybe even corporations to further educate federal lawmakers on the digital tech space, so they can make better-informed decisions. But whether new legislation is drafted to protect children or adults, there remain questions about how to enforce any new laws. Enforcement will arguably be the most significant benefit of any federal bill, but without increased funding or an updated infrastructure, this might be asking a lot of the FTC.

Regulation also raises the question of where to draw the line before we reach the point of diminishing returns and regulations result in unintended consequences that do more harm than good. Technology is like a hammer in that its effectiveness and danger are relative to its use. You can use a hammer as a tool to hit nails, or you can use it as a weapon to do damage. Cybercrime inflicts a tremendous amount of damage, but this technology has also enabled us to connect with family and friends on the other side of the world. It has democratized access to an almost unlimited supply of information, and transformed the way we diagnose and cure diseases. We don't want regulation that limits how this amazing technology can be used as a tool. A balance needs to be struck when figuring out what ecosystem we want to create.

Add all of these factors up and it's unrealistic to expect us to make any legislative progress in the next couple of years. It might be a while before we see that kind of legislative shift, but that doesn't mean things aren't changing and we can't make progress.

## Corporate Accountability

While news and alerts of hacks and data breaches become more common, the good news is that the problem is not entirely falling on deaf ears. The issue of cybersecurity is starting to get people's attention, albeit slowly, but awareness is the first step.

As people become more aware of this issue and how the buying and selling of their data can lead to identity theft and other forms of cybercrime, companies have been forced to change. To avoid bad PR, many apps and websites are giving users a choice to opt out of accepting cookies and other tracking methods.

Data brokers are beginning to feel some heat as well. Between July 2008 and July 2017, Epsilon sold more than 30 million consumers' data to customers they knew were engaged in fraud. That's worth repeating: Epsilon, one of the major data brokers that can legally purchase your data, sold data to third parties they *knew* to be engaged in fraud. In 2021, Epsilon reached a settlement with the DOJ for $150 million for facilitating elder fraud schemes, with $127.5 million of that going to the victims.[3] The settlement also required Epsilon to take further measures to protect consumer data, which includes a process for consumers to request their data not be sold to third parties.

Epsilon isn't the only company being brought to task. Life360 is a location tracking app that allows families to share real-time updates with each other to ensure their safety.

In 2021, they faced scrutiny when two former employees revealed how the company sold the location data for millions of its users to data brokers. That included the location data for children. And it was big business. According to *The Markup*,[4] they made $16 million selling the data for its 33 million users in 2020 alone. That's a substantial increase from the $700,000 they made from selling data in 2016, so the value of this information is growing exponentially. It's a major revenue stream, and it is how company leadership claims they can keep their services free for the customer.

Even after these claims were made public and Life360 agreed to stop selling "precise location data," the company noted it would continue to sell data in aggregate form.[5] On the surface, this feels like an improvement. But, in reality, it is incredibly simple to use easily accessible technology in order to deanonymize data sets.

Life360 is an excellent example of how individuals working within these industries are playing a critical role in bringing these off-color privacy practices into the public debate. Whistleblowers are in the unique position to nudge legislators and public opinion in the right direction by helping to create awareness of the realities of the information economy within large corporations. They can urge the public to seek justice when data brokers, advertisers, companies, and apps abuse customer data. However, we can't put all of our hope in the lone voice of a bold whistleblower.

The most potent driver of change might be big tech itself. Without relying on legislation, Google, Apple, Amazon, and Microsoft can collectively shape how the internet functions to create faster, more effective change. They have the power to regulate what is and is not allowed on their platforms. This gets into a gray area because they continue to profit from data collection. Of course, they will each want to reshape the internet so it aligns with their interests, but that power can be wielded with this bottom-up approach to create short-term change in the right direction.

Many people aren't very hopeful that we'll see a solution from Big Tech regarding privacy and security policies, but we know these major players can work together when there is a common goal. One recent example is the conversation around going passwordless, which is a step that eliminates one layer of vulnerability by allowing users to sign into accounts using biometric data and other methods. This standard was first set by the FIDO (Fast IDentity Online) alliance and the World Wide Web Consortium (W3C). In 2021, Microsoft took the first step toward passwordless accounts with Windows Hello and Microsoft Authenticator. Apple and Google followed suit, and the trend has been supported by chip developers, operating systems, and banking platforms. It's a safer and more secure way to sign into accounts on multiple devices and websites, and that thinking is almost unanimous among those in technical circles. I'm inspired by seeing all of these Big Tech companies work together to make passwordless login capabilities into a reality, and I hope that trend toward features that improve consumer safety will continue.

It will be interesting to see how big tech responds to this growing data privacy concern, because their moves would be the most effective form of short-term change. Maybe they could create something similar to the FIDO alliance for privacy by partnering up and having a technical committee develop recommendations to restructure privacy regulation and the entire data exchange ecosystem. That would be a way to improve the privacy rights of regular citizens in lieu of passing sweeping federal legislation, and since the COVID-19 pandemic began, intervention from Big Tech has become more critical than ever.

## The Need for Improved Employee Protection

When the COVID-19 pandemic took hold and forced workers into home offices, the separation between work and home became nonexistent. Going to the office has been replaced by Zoom meetings. Virtual communication and interaction have become the norm. More companies are letting their employees work from home or are consolidating office space to save on rent. Now, everything is connected. Your home devices are often used for work. Your kids can attend school online using their own devices.

With the new hybrid work model, enterprise security now relies on and depends on individual security. Employees can't take the company firewall and those enterprise digital safety solutions with them outside the office. So, instead of hacking into a more heavily protected company system, cybercriminals can find much easier access to corporate data by going through their less protected remote employees.

It's easy to assume that older employees would be the weak link, but that isn't always the case. A recent study[6] revealed that Gen Z and millennial employees are actually the ones who are less serious about cybersecurity on their work devices, despite having lived with these cyber risks for most of their lives, with 48 percent of Gen Z and 39 percent of millennial employees admitting they don't take cybersecurity as seriously on their work devices as they do on their personal devices.

They are more likely than baby boomers to disregard mandatory IT updates, accept cookies, and use the same passwords as they do on their personal devices.

This takes what was already a growing problem and makes it worse. Companies are left more exposed, and everyday employees have become bigger targets because of the access they can provide hackers.

According to Osterman Research, there is a one-in-four chance that employees will click a link that puts everyone in the company at risk.[7] In 2022, Twilio and Cisco were just two companies that experienced a data breach as a result of an employee phishing attack. And the average cost of detecting and responding to these breaches for companies is going up—from $4.24 million in 2021 to $4.35 million in 2022.[8]

There's also been an increase in CEO spear phishing[9] (hackers spoofing CEO email accounts to trick employees into giving up sensitive information) and hackers posing as IT or HR personnel.[10] Now that employees aren't all working together in the same office, it's easier get away with. At the end of 2022, we saw a trend in cybercriminals creating fake LinkedIn profiles to appear even more authentic when conducting these types of attacks. They also pose as recruiters and create fake job postings to collect personal and financial information from unsuspecting applicants. The fact that LinkedIn is considered the social network for more serious professionals makes it easier for criminals to trick victims because they aren't on the lookout for scams the same way they would be on platforms such as Instagram or Facebook.[11]

This hasn't gone unnoticed. Companies are growing more concerned about the increased security risk that comes with a remote workforce.[12] Many are already investing more in identity theft and privacy solutions for their employees. Some consider it part of a benefits package. Identity theft protection is one of the fastest-growing corporate benefits with 78 percent of employers expected to offer it to employees in 2022. That's up 25 percent from 2021.[13] One reason is because employees are starting to appreciate this benefit and take advantage of it. A survey conducted by the Identity Theft Resource Center (ITRC) and Aura found that two-thirds of employees would use a benefit like this or a free resource. Half would be willing to pay for it themselves.[14]

Not only is this good for employers because it keeps their business safe from digital threats, but it's also the right thing to do because it protects employees who have become more vulnerable to these attacks while working from home. Providing these benefits and free cybersecurity resources can incentivize employees to take a more active approach to their own digital safety, both at work and at home. Hopefully, it will even get them to adapt more preventative and proactive behaviors. As an ancillary benefit, this also pays dividends for the employer. That same ITRC survey revealed that 90 percent of employees became more invested in their company's security as a result of these services and benefits.[15]

In the future, it's easy to see this perk expanding to include protections for the children and families of employees. However, we have a long way to go before all workplaces can bring their remote systems up to speed and protect against ever-evolving digital threats. And companies need to figure out which services and protections best fit their needs, but it's good that we're seeing this become a trend.

In the meantime, many employees who work from home must rely on the average consumer protections, which don't come close to matching what a company can provide. Companies can afford extensive, full-spectrum digital safety solutions, but the individual customer is left with software built for an era before mobile, cloud, big data, and AI. Today, when the average person shops for digital safety solutions, they find many of the exact same options I did back in 2014. And those weren't even new then. The market has been neglected and the consumer left behind. If they want to be protected, they need to figure things out for themselves, and that's no easy task.

## Current Digital Safety Solutions

When the internet was constructed, security wasn't a consideration. It took years of development and iteration before the industry developed a suitable security fabric that could be layered on top of the internet. When the technology progressed to where online security was strong enough to enable online transactions, the floodgates opened. The dot-com boom hit and there was a massive influx of start-ups and an uptick in internet usage, thus creating the need for digital safety.

When the antivirus software industry came into its own in the late 1980s and early 1990s, the internet was a very different place. At first, there were a handful of new viruses a week, and that problem could be addressed manually. An analyst could look at the virus that came out that day to learn how it worked and what steps were needed to remove it. Even when there were a few new viruses daily, this could all be done with a few humans, but the number of viruses has increased significantly. Today, more than a million new viruses and threats are created every day, but the infrastructure in place was built to solve the problem manually.

As the nature of the threat changed, the industry addressed it by throwing more people at the problem. They added more hands to do the manual labor, but soon realized that this wasn't an issue that could realistically be addressed by hand. That's when they started looking for more advanced ways to detect and eliminate viruses. The result is the antivirus software on the market today, but how well does that protect the average consumer?

If you look closely at most consumer antivirus software, it's enterprise software that's been given a shiny coat of paint so it can be repurposed for the consumer. It does what it promises, but that promise is limited, and it doesn't make digital life any easier. If anything, consumers tend to have a lot of complaints because it can interfere with how their system operates. One reason is that much of what's included in this software isn't necessary for the average consumer. The features might be useful to a highly technical customer looking for tech to enable specific online behaviors, but they'll never be used by the vast majority of people. That said, these added bells and whistles give companies an excuse to charge an extra couple of bucks. Unfortunately, consumers haven't had a choice to save on these premiums, because with the abundance of digital threats, antivirus software is absolutely essential if you want to do anything online.

When online shopping and banking became common, monitoring services emerged to alert consumers of threats. Credit alerts became popular. This is a note placed on a credit report that requires verification from the individual before any additional lines of credit can be issued. It's free and can go far in preventing identity theft. A credit lock takes this even further and flat-out prevents any new lines of credit from being issued because lenders can't access a customer's credit history. It's more of a hassle to set up because it requires enrolling in a program with each of three major credit bureaus, and it prevents the customer from opening up a new line of credit until the lock is removed, but it's more secure.

Credit monitoring is also essential these days, and if used properly, it can be a lifesaver. Before he was a member, John received a letter from a car dealership in Oklahoma saying that his credit was denied. He had a common name, so he assumed there was an honest mix-up, and he forgot about it. The following week, he received a similar letter from another dealership in Texas. That's when he got nervous and signed up for credit monitoring, but the floodgates were already open, so he immediately received an alert from another car dealership, this time in Arkansas.

John immediately phoned the dealership and learned they had just shipped an Aston Martin in his name to some address in Little Rock. His next call was to the Little Rock Police Department, which sent officers to meet and arrest the thieves when the car was delivered. Had he not signed up for credit monitoring, the thieves might have gotten away with it, and he could have been on the hook for the charges. Since he caught it early, he was able to clear his credit for the purchase and the inquiries before any real damage was done. The experience left him riddled with anxiety and is the reason why he eventually signed up for Aura.

Despite the general public becoming more aware of the need for digital safety, most responsible and informed people still don't take the time to educate themselves about the risk and the process of remediation until they are directly impacted. In my experience, there tends to be a significant knowledge gap between those who have experienced identity theft and fraud versus those who have not. The average person doesn't have the time to learn the ins and outs of digital safety and how they are at risk, unless they need to. But, as I've said a few times, it's much easier to prevent a problem from occurring than trying to fix it after the fact. In my many conversations with people who have been victims of online criminals, I've met too many people who find themselves dealing with the fallout of theft because they aren't informed about what they need to do to prevent it from happening in the first place.

The products and services we use, whether Apple, Google, Verizon, or dozens of others, provide some protection, but not nearly enough. In a perfect world, these companies would all work together and collaborate to provide the best protection possible, but there is so much fragmentation, and every company has its own agenda to protect. Because of that, these companies don't have your best interest in mind—they have their own. That is why you need a third party, but what are your options today?

Many people already use antivirus software, credit monitoring, parental controls, privacy tools, password managers, dark web monitoring, and identity theft protection services, and some of them are really good. These services are becoming more popular, and there is no better indication of that than by looking at how many of them there are. The market is saturated, and while choice is good, it has only exacerbated the problem by adding an additional level of complexity to an already confusing topic. There are now so many digital security products that customers don't know how to differentiate one from the other. But there is an even bigger problem facing the customer.

Despite all of these products, there is still no one place where customers can go to get all the modern tools they need to protect themselves and their families. Security vendors tend to offer single solutions to single threats, so you would have to spend about eighty dollars in monthly subscription fees for six different services to receive comprehensive protection and cover all your digital vulnerabilities.

That requires a massive effort to research and understand all your options, so you know which products you can trust. And if you choose wrong, the software might slow down your device. Unfortunately, many people don't get that far because they feel so overwhelmed by all the solutions available on the market that they don't know where to start. It's paralysis by analysis, so they end up doing nothing, or worse, relying on the same security techniques they used ten or twenty years ago. That leaves them reusing the same passwords and not taking the time to implement multi-factor authentication. They're left dancing around a cyber minefield, and any false step could blow a hole in their level of security.

That risk will only increase in the years to come as more of your family's work, money, and health care transition online. As the digital world evolves faster, we get stuck in a cycle of perpetually having to play catch-up with our solutions because every cool new gadget comes with an alarming new threat. You don't want to make the same mistake as many others and wait for the catastrophic digital event to occur before protecting yourself. Luckily, you don't have to because there is finally that all-in-one solution that keeps you and your family safe. It's simple, easy to use, and there hasn't been anything like it before.

# CHAPTER 5

# A New Paradigm: Intelligent Safety

Once your information is on the dark web, it's out there, making you more susceptible to additional attacks. I discovered that firsthand, but luckily, I had learned my lesson and was already working on a solution, so when it happened again, I was prepared.

At the beginning of the pandemic, there was a lot of confusion about what to do and what not to do. There was talk of government assistance for individuals and PPP loans for businesses to help them navigate the downturn. Our company didn't apply for a loan, but I received an alert from my personal Aura account that there was an inquiry for a PPP loan on my credit.

Having been a victim of identity theft only a few years earlier, and after everything I learned about cybercrime and how scammers prey on vulnerability and confusion during disasters, I still didn't understand the initial implications. Even when you know the warning signs, it's easy not to put two and two together. My first instinct was to think that our engineers were testing a new feature. However, I knew enough to check with my team, who told me they weren't running a test. That meant this was a real inquiry into my credit.

I called the PPP loan office in Texas, and they pulled up a loan application for $70,000 submitted for Aura, which was listed as a car dealership in Texas. It wasn't a real company, but the scammers had gone so far as to create a fake website and bank account for the dealership before applying for the loan. They even asked the PPP office to directly wire them the funds.

It took a couple of phone calls, but I could clear up the issue before any damage was done. Had I not received that Aura alert and informed the PPP office of the fraud, they would have approved the loan, wired the money to the criminals, and then come to us a few months later looking to collect. It would have been much harder to resolve and certainly would've required more than a few phone calls. There is a chance we would have been responsible for that money. This was during a time when we were still growing, and for a start-up of our size, that would have been a major blow.

This feature isn't unique to Aura. Had I turned on an Experian credit alert, I would have gotten the same exact warning. It's crucial that Aura caught this, and I was able to prevent any further damage, but traditional technology couldn't stop this from happening. It was another fire alarm. It got me thinking: how much better would it be if this didn't happen at all? What if this process of fraud identification could be automated? That is the idea behind a whole new category of digital safety called intelligent safety.

While our safety precautions could once focus almost entirely on our physical surroundings, we live an increasingly online, connected life. So today, our digital life is our real life. Over the years, we've heard a lot about the concepts of safety, cybersecurity, digital security, and digital wellness. Intelligent safety extends beyond the scope of any of those practices. What makes intelligent safety different from past approaches to online safety is that it's driven by artificial intelligence (AI), so it can proactively protect you as a unique individual. We think of it as a guardian or shield that insulates you both online and off.

As the lines separating the physical from the digital start to blur, there is no going back. Pretty soon, those lines might not exist at all, and we need a modern safety solution that reflects that reality. Aura is the first to offer this type of intelligent safety product, but we don't want to be the only company with these solutions. We want others to follow our lead because this is an area where there is room for tremendous innovation.

Intelligent safety is the first step to creating a safer internet, and it's a category of protection that I hope will continue to grow along with technology and the nature of cyber threats. The future of digital protection will adapt to your needs, so it can prevent problems before they even occur. Intelligent safety makes things simple and easy, so you don't have to worry about insulating your family from the threats in the connected world. Let the technology do that for you and enjoy the peace of mind that comes with knowing your family can safely enjoy all the conveniences of the internet.

## Intelligent Safety in Action

Prevention, detection, and response are the three levels of digital safety. They all need to be strong because if something slips through the cracks of one level, you want the threat to be eliminated when it reaches the next.

The first and arguably most crucial level is prevention. The fewer digital threats you have to deal with, the better. It's good to have a doctor help bring you back to good health, but it would be so much better to not get sick in the first place. Intelligent safety is that preventative protection because it can see around digital corners to spot those telltale patterns of an attack before they occur.

Lauren's SIM swap from the first chapter is the perfect example of how intelligent safety can be so effective. This type of attack targets multiple points of vulnerability, but had she been using intelligent safety, those vulnerabilities would have been shored up, so the cybercriminal wouldn't have been able to execute the attack.

First, her personal information would not have been out on the internet for someone to find. If her login credentials had been stolen, the system would have updated them automatically. A credit alert would have immediately informed her of any new inquiry on her credit from a mobile provider and given her the option to lock or freeze it to stop the attempt in its tracks. This is how these features work together to prevent attacks from ever occurring. That is the best line of defense, and it's what makes intelligent safety so effective, but given the nature of cyber threats, we have to assume that at some point in your life, the water in your digital pipes will leak.

You could do everything right and have the most advanced digital security, but no product will prevent every threat before it occurs. You can be a conscientious driver who follows all the rules of the road and still wind up in an accident through no fault of your own. Digital threats work the same way, and like cars have seat belts, airbags, and a slew of safety features to protect you and your family, intelligent safety is equally good at detecting the threats that do occur, so you can quickly respond before any damage is done.

Another benefit of machine learning is that it can be used to detect new threats the instant they become an issue for consumers, whereas legacy technology stacks could take days, weeks, or even months to deliver similar insights. It gives intelligent safety a head start when shutting down scammers before they can do significant damage. That's important, because 40 percent of the fraudulent activity that results from an account takeover occurs within one day.[1]

Every second counts when it comes to stopping fraud. Intelligent safety can quickly step in to clean up any problems, whether clawing back stolen data or alerting credit bureaus of fraud. With one click, you can lock your credit to protect yourself if someone tries to open credit cards or take out loans in your name. You'll get real-time alerts if someone tries to access your credit file when it's locked. Those alerts could prompt you to make simple changes that take only seconds but can save you weeks, if not months, if the problem wasn't caught early.

Before signing up for intelligent safety, James received a notification that his information was included in a data breach of a major rideshare service. He quickly logged on, changed his username and password, and then forgot about it. A few weeks later, he received an email informing him his Hulu password had changed. A second alert soon followed, saying that his language preference on Hulu had been changed from English to French. When he sat down at his computer to look into the issue, he received another email. His Amazon password had changed. He was starting to get nervous. Now locked out of multiple accounts, he was faced with the daunting task of proving his own identity.

James was vulnerable because his rideshare, Hulu, and Amazon accounts all had the same password. Even though he quickly changed the rideshare password when he received the first notification, the damage had already been done. Scammers know that people reuse the same passwords, so once they get ahold of one, they try to use it to access your other accounts. And a lot of times, it works. We see this happen all the time. Ninety-one percent of people know that reusing the same password puts their online security at risk, yet 66 percent still do it.[2]

Let's imagine this same scenario if James had already set up his intelligent safety protections. He would have received an alert that his credentials had been found on the dark web. Within that alert, he would see if he had similar credentials for other accounts in his password manager. The intelligent safety system would offer to automatically update all of these at-risk passwords for him, so the leak in James' cybersecurity pipes would be immediately patched.

Most users don't understand how the technology behind intelligent safety is different. Some might not even care how AI solves this large swath of potential problems, but that doesn't matter. Whether they're interested or not, the goal remains to deliver a positive, intuitive experience.

For intelligent safety to truly be a benefit, it needs to be accessible and easy to use. Artificial intelligence, machine learning, and all the corresponding data help set the technology apart, but it doesn't do the public any good if you need a degree in computer science to operate the system. That's why we designed intelligent safety to be effortless. You don't need to know anything about technology to use it. Just direct us with a few taps and clicks, and our system does the rest. No hassle. No worry. That's true intelligent safety. That's possible because artificial intelligence connects all the various components of digital safety, allowing them to work together to meet the specific needs of you and your family.

## Artificial Intelligence: The Backbone of Intelligent Safety

Internet security is not a monolith; it's a mosaic. There are so many threats out there, and they all have nuances and subtleties that traditional digital safety products weren't designed to combat. Intelligent safety brings together internet security, privacy tools, and identity theft solutions, which up until now, had to be implemented and operated separately. It takes each one beyond the one-size-fits-all digital safety patches currently offered to customers and personalizes them to fit your needs. Our goal is to make our security service smarter than the hackers trying to breach it. The way we do that is to address these problems holistically with artificial intelligence and data.

It may seem like AI is an obvious way to solve this problem, but that wasn't always the case. You need a team of people who understand how machine learning systems, cybercrime, and malware work, but there just aren't that many people who work at that intersection. This is getting more common today, but it's one reason why a solution like this hasn't taken off before, and why we made sure to assemble the right team who could execute this ambitious vision.

By taking this data-driven approach, digital solutions can be more accurate and spot meaningful patterns that could escape human eyes; patterns that require computational horsepower to detect. In a world where we see new malware developed every day, AI allows us to scale beyond what we can manually monitor and detect.

Most threats involve more than one activity. To address those threats requires looking at the entire ecosystem or the chain of events that could unfold throughout a threat. Because the different components of intelligent safety are unified, they communicate and work together in ways that wouldn't occur if you were forced to cobble together different solutions for different problems from different companies. Intelligent safety takes data from all of these different areas and stitches it together to create even more meaningful data. By bringing all of these services together on a single platform and building AI capabilities into the services, it can enable new security features that were not previously possible. That creates more value for the individual.

Machine learning allows the systems to not only adapt to the ever-changing nature of these threats but also adapt to the user and their individual risk level. Intelligent safety systems learn the unique ways you might be at risk from your interactions and work with you to increasingly personalize the type of protection it provides.

Everyone is different. Their online habits are different, which makes their vulnerabilities different. Some people do more online shopping than others, some rely more heavily on their online banking app, and others only use their laptop for transactions. Intelligent safety adapts to fit your needs. It also changes in real time as your life, the tech landscape, and the nature of these digital threats change. This keeps you ahead of scammers to ensure you're protected. That's important in a world with emerging platforms and an almost endless stream of new connected devices.

Here are some of the common problems that technology like intelligent safety can prevent:

## Leaked Login Credentials

Not only is a password manager a secure and efficient way to store all of your online passwords so you don't need to memorize (or even know) them, but it's even more effective when it's used in conjunction with other digital safety features. This is one of the best examples of intelligent safety in action.

Let's say the system sees that a user's account has been breached on the dark web; the AI can review the password linked to that account to assess the risk. It can then look into the user's password manager to identify any other accounts that might use a similar password and automatically update them on both the at-risk site and within the user's password manager for future use. This way, even if cybercriminals get ahold of your password, they can't do anything with it. If you have two different services to perform those functions, they aren't sharing data and can't make those connections to protect you.

Beyond the password management use case, similar concepts are being explored for family protections. For example, a family vault, where one person could store and share sensitive documents with family members in a way that allows them to choose who has permission to access that information. This could include Social Security numbers, birth certificates, home titles, medical records, financial information, vaccine cards, or insurance documents.

Let's take it a step further. What if every time you scan something sensitive, the family vault could analyze the document and suggest whether it should be stored in the shared family vault? A service like this could become a useful guide. If it sees you haven't included your home title, the system could make that suggestion. If you reach a certain age and don't have a will in the vault, the system could suggest you consider starting those plans. That's not just assisting; it's true intelligence and a glimpse at what might soon be possible with this technology.

## Malicious Websites

When building Aura, we had access to this massive data set of VPN (virtual private network) information. We then combined that information to identify patterns and anomalies in website traffic. Because of that, we know for a fact that most scams occur on websites that were created in the previous forty-eight hours.

That type of data is used to create intelligent safety's smart network. Most fraudulent scam sites are spun up and abandoned within forty-eight hours, making the date when the website was published a key indicator as to whether a website is safe or not. Traditionally, this information has been moderated manually, but given the speed with which the sites are created and abandoned, manual approaches will never be sufficient. It often takes days to identify and block malicious sites manually. By that point, there is no value in blocking the site, as the attacker has already moved on.

With intelligent safety, this data check is automated for users through machine learning. So, when you go to a website, the system will automatically look at specific features to see when the account was registered and developed. If it sees the site was created twelve hours earlier and is now asking for your credit card information, it can be reasonably certain that your personal or financial information is at risk and can block your access to the site to prevent you from walking into a trap. Right now, these scam sites might not be detected and removed for up to two months because that process is entirely manual. By the time many are detected, they have already been inactive for weeks.

In addition to the safe browsing features, the intelligent safety system can turn on the VPN to keep your data safe every time you connect to a potentially unsafe public network, whether at a Starbucks or the airport. The built-in VPN is encrypted, so it hides your online activity from cybercriminals. That lets you shop, bank, and stream online content privately and securely, no matter where you are.

## Scam Phone Calls

Robocalls and spam texts are pretty high on people's list of annoyances. Some people may have gotten used to them as a way of life, but that doesn't need to be the case.

This is another example of how data can be so powerful because, based on prior intelligence about any given phone number, the intelligent safety system can pre-filter callers known to be the source of spam phone calls. If it sees that multiple customers received spam phone calls from a specific phone number, the system can automatically block that number. But, even using that technology and collective intelligence, calls can still get through, which is why a second line of defense is built in.

If you receive a call from a number that isn't in your contacts, a spam call assistant can answer those calls for you and engage with the caller automatically. It can then do two things. The AI speech recognition processes and analyzes the natural language to detect if the caller's intent is legitimate. If it's a bot or a criminal using a known scam script, that call will be sent directly to voicemail and automatically marked as spam. It also creates a transcript, so if it can't positively determine if the call is legitimate, it can send you that transcript to help you decide whether you want to take the call. This works the same exact way for text messages.

The major benefit of working with AI is that it doesn't look at content in isolation. It can factor in both the content (the number itself) and the context (the response or text). Combine these two, and the system can more accurately determine the legitimacy of a phone call or text message. That's so incredibly important when creating these proactive solutions.

## The Benefits of Intelligent Safety for Parents

Keeping your kids safe online is daunting, but intelligent safety can serve as an easy button, so you don't need to constantly look over their shoulders or keep tabs on what they're doing.

While a smart network is an excellent tool for parents because it allows them to determine which sites are appropriate for kids, machine learning can also be designed to look for curse words or inappropriate content. It then compiles data and harnesses the power of AI to perform content filtering for kids.

What's great about the algorithm is that it can catch things a human can't see. Sure, you can look at a website to determine if the text passes the eye test, but what you don't know is the IP address or where the site is hosted. If a site is known for malicious content, the algorithm can weed that out. And if the system hasn't seen the site or something like it before, that's usually a sign that it's not legitimate.

What sets intelligent safety apart is the intuitive parental controls you can customize on all your children's devices based on their age, interests, and what you deem appropriate. These are easy to set up and manage. The database bundles millions of websites into easy-to-understand categories, so you can filter by category or individual websites, platforms, apps, and streaming services. Let's say you want to allow access to Instagram but block TikTok. That can be done with the click of a button. If you don't want your kids to visit dating sites, that's another click. This goes beyond the typical one-size-fits-all approach with other parental control systems. Managing what your kids can access online becomes easy, and you can customize these filters to fit every child in your family because they each have their own accounts.

Screen time limits work the same way. Kids between the ages of eight and eighteen spend 7.5 hours a day in front of a screen, which can significantly impact their development and productivity.[3] With intelligent safety, you can customize limits for different apps and websites to check if your child has been scrolling too long. Monitoring their activity helps you set fair limits in the future without feeling like you're intruding on their privacy or taking away their independence. For you, it's like putting a timer on the internet, so you know your kids aren't overdoing it or bingeing YouTube when they should be studying or sleeping.

Your kids will also have the same protections shared by every adult family member. Their computers and phones are secured with the same antivirus software and VPN. It doesn't matter if they are at home, school, or at a friend's house; they will be safe when online. You have the comfort of knowing your kids have the same identity theft protection and social security monitoring. You'll get real-time alerts if there are signs of fraud, so you won't be blindsided.

One of the most forward-thinking features is the toxic interaction detection. If your child is a regular gamer, intelligent safety systems can use artificial intelligence to analyze voice and text conversations to detect unhealthy situations, including sexual harassment, cyberbullying, grooming, and racism.

In the future, a feature like this might be applied to your kids' entire online experience. The challenge once again comes back to context because the conversations occurring when your kid is playing *Call of Duty* with a group of friends is drastically different than what might be considered acceptable when posting on Instagram. The words *shoot, gun,* and *kill* might be frequent when playing *Call of Duty* yet considered threatening on Instagram. Making that distinction requires understanding the statistical properties of the data and comparing it to what is the norm for the context. So, *Call of Duty* would have a much different model for dangerous content identification than Instagram posts.

As a parent, intelligent safety can do much of this heavy lifting for you, and the future possibilities are vast, but whether designing the system for adults or kids, there are challenges regarding how the AI maneuvers through the digital landscape.

## Overcoming the Challenges of a Proactive Approach

Let's go back to the credit alert I received about someone taking out a PPP loan using my personal information. In a perfect world, the AI could identify the legitimacy of new credit inquiries based on recent web history and transactions. Intelligent safety could take that next proactive step that other services could not and implement an automatic credit freeze at first sight of any strange activity. But before the technology can become truly autonomous, there are some regulatory hurdles we need to overcome as a society. For example, our recovery team can't make calls to the credit bureaus on the customers' behalf. The customer needs to be on the line to authorize us to speak on their behalf.

We have agreements with the credit bureaus that provide critical information for us to protect individuals, but there are restrictions in their contracts that say what we can do with it. As you know, every state has a different set of requirements. We need to ensure we comply with all of them, which gets complex. The type of data that can be shared among family members can change from state to state. Some states may require power of attorney. Others require notarized signatures. Some don't have those same restrictions. It's common for spouses to know or at least have access to each other's Social Security numbers, but as soon as you facilitate the sharing of that information directly through the software, you need to be careful from a legal perspective.

Even more challenging than navigating the legal landscape is dealing with a constantly changing threat. Cybercriminals aren't static adversaries. Instead of shooting at a stationary target, it's like we're shooting at one that is erratic and always moving. Our adversaries constantly adapt, morph, and switch up their techniques to make money and avoid detection.

It's the brand-new attacks that pose the biggest challenge for machine learning systems, simply because there is no data history the system can draw from. This applies to new games, software platforms, and even new users.

There will always be a margin for error when dealing with these zero-day problems. However, with AI, you can better control the type of errors the system makes at first and speed the process of adapting to new threats.

Errors go in two directions. The system either labels something bad when it's good or it labels something good when it's bad. When dealing with an unknown, the AI is forced to make a guess, but you can control which way the error goes. That choice depends entirely on the scenario.

Let's say you're working for the federal government and are in charge of providing digital security for a nuclear power plant when you come across a potential threat you know nothing about. The data might indicate a 25 percent chance it's legitimate, but given the situation, you can't take the risk of being wrong. In that case, you need the AI to take a guilty until proven innocent approach, so you program it to shut everything down.

The approach will probably be completely different if you're dealing with robocalls. You can program the system to let a few calls through the filter because, in this situation, it's better to be wrong and let a few robocalls slip through the filter than to automatically block real calls that the AI doesn't immediately recognize. Then, you can course correct later when the system better understands the nature of the threat.

Further, it's possible to add an entirely new set of data to the mix in the form of user feedback. This could help create an additional layer of accuracy. For example, let's say that a spam text gets through. The system can take that input and feed it back into the algorithm. That would allow it to continually update the system and better understand the nature of potential threats. In other words, that data can help the system better figure out what's good and what's bad.

When the AI spots these scams in advance, it can proactively warn customers. For example, suppose some users accidentally downloaded malware from a specific site and subsequently experienced some financial impact because it exfiltrated their bank account credentials. In that case, the system can proactively mitigate that risk for others who might have downloaded that same malware by locking their credit or freezing their accounts.

One of the challenges of working with AI is having to infer intent. That's something we, as humans, struggle with. Every day, we make incorrect assumptions about people. We misunderstand and misinterpret people all the time. Expecting an AI to make all decisions perfectly right out of the gate is not reasonable, but we try to do our best and decide which type of error we prefer to make in each situation. But what's so beneficial about AI is that it's much easier to change a behavior because it quickly learns and adapts with access to the right data. That's why data is so important.

Machine learning is not about fancy algorithms. It's about data because you can't make meaningful inferences without good data. Just like you can't make good wine from poor grapes, we need that quality data to serve as our foundational starting point. And we constantly update the model with new data to make it more accurate. With the combination of the right data, and intelligent safety being used properly, you should not fall victim to financial fraud or identity theft because these problems will be proactively prevented or solved without you having to intervene.

## The User Experience

Most of the digital safety services on the market act like smoke detectors. They alert you of the problem when it arises, and you're the one who has to go do something about it. From the beginning, intelligent safety was designed to be the fire suppression system that prevents the problem from developing by reducing the risk.

Everyone has a different level of trust in technology. No two families are the same, and even individuals within a given family have a different understanding of the digital world. Alerts and guidance that one person might find informative, another might find excessive. This is another area where machine learning and data come into play because we can use that data to better understand and design the customer experience. Similar to how everyone's digital usage and level of risk are different, so are their user preferences. A feature that one person would like to unfold automatically, another would like to be notified of or have more control over the process. If the protection we provide is going to be personalized, it only makes sense that the experience, and the way you interact with intelligent safety, are personalized as well.

Some people need time to learn the technology and become comfortable with the service. When it proves useful, they then feel okay with taking their hands off the wheel and allowing more changes to occur in the background. The service can adapt, and we can tailor the experience according to what resonates with you. What bucket you fall into depends on your understanding of the tech and desired level of control.

The digitally savvy might not require the same notifications as a frazzled parent who doesn't have the same understanding of technology and deeply desires more visibility into his family's tech habits.

I want you and your family to do everything you want to do online without worrying or compromising convenience. I want you to take advantage of technology without it taking advantage of you. It doesn't matter your age, understanding of technology, or where you're coming from; I want to educate people on the nature of digital threats, how they are at risk, and what they can do to mitigate that risk. That's why our team continually looks for innovative ways to connect those dots, so we can achieve our goal of making the internet a safer place.

It was precisely this kind of simple, all-in-one, proactive personal protection I was looking for after my identity was stolen. That's why I couldn't be more excited to see this vision finally come to fruition. I'm proud to offer families protection that allows them to take back control and spend their time focused on what's most important in life.

# PART 2
# Protecting Your Connected Family

The main goal of almost every cybercriminal is to get your money.

There are hundreds of ways to defraud you and just as many digital vulnerabilities that can be exploited. Without the proper protections, the money in your bank account, your credit, and your financial security are in jeopardy. Make just one mistake when it comes to your digital safety, and the consequences can be disastrous, but it doesn't need to be that way. By understanding how you're vulnerable, and the simple habits you can adopt to protect yourself, you can exponentially decrease the chance of falling victim to fraud or identity theft. And with protections such as intelligent safety, you further insulate yourself and limit the damage because you have a guardian and a partner who is right there with you if something goes wrong.

However, our customers aren't only worried about themselves and their money. They, like me, are concerned about their families. They have aging parents who are prime targets for cybercriminals. In 2021, 92,371 Americans over sixty were victims of fraud and suffered a cumulative loss of $1.7

billion—a 70 percent increase from the year before. That's an average of $18,246 per victim and the highest dollar amount among any age-group.[1] Scammers will use anything they can think of to trick the elderly. We've seen them target the confusion surrounding Medicare and reverse mortgages to con people into sharing sensitive information. Some of the boldest con them into believing their grandchildren are in danger and get them to send money.

If your parents don't know what to look out for, they might lose the nest egg they worked so hard their entire lives to earn. Even though you can't look over your parents' shoulders, you can provide them with the proper protections that fit their specific needs, and then rest assured they won't be duped.

In addition to expressing concern about their aging parents, our customers ask us about one topic more than any other: how they can protect their children.

I have four children and they are all connected. I think it's amazing what they are able to do with technology. They surprise me with their creativity across the different apps and games they play every day, but that doesn't mean I don't worry. My concerns are the same as those I hear from customers all the time. Which social media platforms are collecting my children's data? Which platforms expose them to potential scams? Who are my kids really talking to while gaming? What kind of content are they seeing on TikTok? How do I know if my child is being cyberbullied, and how can I intervene?

Many parents don't know the answers to these questions. They understand that there are dangers their children face online, but they aren't familiar enough with the landscape to know exactly what those dangers are or what to do about them. And, I'm going to let you all in on a secret—even if you live and breathe security and privacy, it's nearly impossible to keep up with the risk landscape facing kids.

But, you don't have to feel like you're totally in the dark anymore. What follows is a crash course to bring you up to speed on how your children spend their time online, what behaviors can make them vulnerable, and what safety measures you can put in place to protect them. You will also get tips on talking to your kids, so you can come to a mutual understanding without making them feel like you're spying on them or trying to take away their digital freedoms.

Every family dynamic is different, and what works for one family might not be best for yours. Luckily, you can use many tools and resources to find the best way to protect your loved ones because there is no silver bullet or one thing you can do to prevent cybercrime. Developing good online habits and behaviors, and by being proactive and involved in what your children are doing online is the best first step. Combine that with the proper comprehensive protections, and every family can be truly safe.

# CHAPTER 6

# The Secret Lives (and Risks) of Connected Kids

The internet is an excellent way for kids to learn about the world. Today, they have access to information and resources many of us couldn't dream of growing up. But the internet isn't only a resource; it's become ingrained in how kids live, learn, and interact socially.

Independence is taking on a new dimension for the younger generation. While kids used to look forward to getting their driver's license at sixteen or finally becoming an adult at eighteen, new rites of passage have developed in recent years. On average, kids with a smartphone receive it before the age of eight and even those who don't expect to get one before the age of thirteen.[1] The phone is only the beginning. After that comes social media, gaming, and many other online apps. Much of the socialization that once occurred through face-to-face interaction in the real world now happens online or through devices. In many cases, digital independence has become just as valuable to kids as real-world independence.

There's been a lengthy debate about how much time children should spend online. Opinions vary on what is healthy and if too much time spent on devices can limit social development and interpersonal skills. There are many variables to consider, and no two kids are the same, but what is clear is that children are spending more time online than ever before. Roughly 95 percent of American teens have smartphones, and 45 percent claim they are constantly online.[2]

There is no question that technology can help families thrive, but as with everything else online, this comes at the price of our safety and security. So, the more time kids spend online, the more vulnerable they become. It doesn't matter how old your children are; there are multiple dangers they will be exposed to. And the reality is that while we go to great lengths to provide for our families and protect our kids in the real world, when it comes to online life, we're doing much less. And it's not because we don't care. The opposite is true, as 93 percent of parents feel obligated to protect their children online.[3] The problem is that we don't know *what* we can do. It's common for parents to feel scared and powerless, especially when kids seem more familiar and comfortable than we do with the latest devices and technology.

If we want to protect our children online, it begins with becoming more familiar with the playing field. And there is no bigger playing field, and area of concern for parents, than social media.

## The Potential Dangers of Social Media

Former NFL wide receiver Eric Decker didn't think twice before giving his four-year-old son, Forrest, his phone to watch *The Avengers* while he took a shower. However, Forrest didn't watch *The Avengers*. Instead, he took a selfie in the bathroom with his dad visible in the shower behind him and then posted that photo to his dad's Instagram account.

This is a harmless, although somewhat embarrassing, example of what can happen when kids get hold of a smartphone and have access to social media, but there are other, much more serious ways this can go wrong. In only a few minutes, kids can make purchases, buy video games and movies, look up all types of inappropriate content, and interact with people trying to trick them into giving away their personal and financial information.

Social media is where kids go to post, comment, live chat, and stream videos, but it is also a virtual playground for criminals to gather information. Kids may be digital natives and confident about their online knowledge, but that doesn't make them immune to cybercrime. Your children's information can be sold on the dark web, used to commit identity theft, and featured in targeted attacks against them and you. And most of this can be done with the information children willingly put online. This includes name, email, birthplace, and birthday. If your child is excited about earning their driver's license, make sure they understand the dangers of posting a picture of it online. The information from their license allows scammers to send your kids precise phishing emails or use it to commit identity theft.

Not all social media platforms are created equal. Each one has different risks and threats. TikTok is the most popular social media platform for teens, followed by Instagram and Snapchat. Gen Z relies on TikTok as a search engine more than Google, which is an issue since it's much more likely to contain misinformation.[4] Eighty-six percent of teens who use TikTok and Snapchat say they are on both daily. One-fourth of those claim to be on it constantly. TikTok is particularly popular among teen girls compared to teen boys, who gravitate more toward YouTube, Twitch, and Reddit.[5]

What TikTok has been scrutinized for lately is how much data they harvest, and it's probably more than you might think. It includes the videos watched, commented on, key-logger info, phone hardware data, phone GPS location, IP address, browsing history, in-app message content, clipboard data, contacts on the phone and social networks, demographic info, phone number, photos, videos, payment information, private messages, information from any linked social media accounts, and any information provided when creating the account.[6] That's important to consider because the platform is not unhackable, and TikTok doesn't put a priority on user privacy. At the end of 2022, it was revealed that TikTok might have breached UK privacy laws by processing data for children under thirteen without parental consent. It faced fines of up to $29 million.[7]

It's not just your kid's information that is at risk of being stolen. Social media is a breeding ground for scams. In 2021, teens reported close to fifteen thousand online scam incidents[8] and those under the age of twenty were scammed out of $101.4 million.[9] Given how many scams went unreported, that number is probably much higher.

Both Snapchat and Instagram have become popular hangouts for hackers and scammers. These scams come in different forms, but they have two primary objectives: obtain sensitive personal information or trick people into sending money.

Snapchat claims that social engineering attacks are the most common way that hackers take over accounts,[10] but romance and catfish scams are also popular on Snapchat as it's often a preferred platform that scammers use to communicate with victims after they've met them on a dating site.

Meanwhile, many fake Instagram accounts are set up to lure unsuspecting victims with promises of sponsorships, fake merchandise scams, giveaways, get-rich-quick schemes, crypto mining scams, and phony job postings. While phishing scams and account takeovers are common, many kids on Instagram are trying to build a following as influencers or get noticed as musicians, so there are plenty of promotion scams being peddled by fraudsters to prey on young people's hopes and dreams.

What's even more frightening is who your kids might talk to online. There are an estimated five hundred thousand predators online who specifically target young children.[11] These people create fake social media profiles and pretend to be the same age to build an online relationship with your child. Most predators try to get personal very quickly through flattery. They might start by asking private questions, then reveal what appears to be personal information of their own, or try to pressure your child into sending photos, which is a whole different and disturbing area of concern.

Sexting, or sharing nudes, is the act of sending sexually explicit photographs or messages online. What's troubling is that sexting is prevalent among those thirteen to seventeen years old, with two in five teens in this age range saying that it's normal to share nude pictures.[12] Whether parents like it or not, sexting has become a part of adolescent culture, but it's a recipe for disaster. This becomes a crime when an adult convinces a minor to share sexual pictures or perform sexual acts on a webcam. And, unfortunately, it's probably more common than you realize. Twenty-five percent of kids aged nine to seventeen said that an adult had sent or asked them for nude photos.

Parents have a reason to be scared about what their kids might be up to when on social media, but any attempt to get your kid to quit is probably a losing battle that is not worth fighting. Ninety percent of households with children and internet access say those children are on social media.[13] And according to a Pew Research Center survey, 54 percent of teens say it would be hard for them to give up social media.[14] The best line of defense is making sure your children know the dangers that exist and taking the proper preventative actions, so these problems don't even occur.

Here is a list of some basic principles for you and your kids to follow when on social media:

1. Start with strict privacy settings. Keep your kids' profiles private and tell them only to accept friend requests from people they know. Disable location sharing, and limit commenting and posting publicly.

2. Limit the information they provide when signing up for an account. Just because a field is offered in the "about" section doesn't mean it needs to be filled in. And if they want to fill in something, keep it broad. Even adults often forget that harmless information in these sections can often be used to crack password security questions.

3. Make sure they never post or give out personal, financial, or login information. And they should never click

any links. Try to get your kids in the habit of sharing as little information as possible.

4.  Never send inappropriate or compromising photos. A good rule of thumb is that kids shouldn't share photos with anyone on social media or in online forums that they wouldn't want you to see.

5.  Instill in your kids the importance of absolutely never, under any circumstances, agreeing to meet someone they met online in person.

These principles don't only apply to social media but also to another popular area of the internet that can expose them to a different set of dangers and vulnerabilities—online gaming.

## The World of Online Gaming

Online gaming is immensely popular among kids and teenagers. Three-quarters of US households have some sort of gaming device.[15] Gaming is a multibillion-dollar industry and has changed significantly over the years. These games are realistic, immersive, and allow kids to play and communicate with others around the globe in real time.

Online gaming communities continue to grow and can be an excellent way for shy and reserved kids to break out of their shells and socialize with those who have like-minded interests. Gaming can positively impact a child's emotional, cognitive, and social skills while helping them improve their creativity and develop problem-solving skills.

There is considerable overlap between social media and gaming, as many prominent gamers use social media to promote their brand and accounts. Some of the ways users can be exploited are also the same. As with social media, hacking is a concern. In October 2021, almost all of the source code for the gaming platform Twitch was leaked online, including information belonging to seven million of its users.[16] That's why it's crucial that kids follow the same precautions they would on social media and limit the amount of information they provide when setting up accounts.

Despite the apparent similarities, there are just as many, if not more, instances of how gaming and social media differ, specifically in the type of people that populate these platforms and the potential vulnerabilities that leave users exposed. Much attention has been paid to the violence of some video games, particularly first-person shooter games such as *Fortnite*, *Call of Duty*, and *Grand Theft Auto*. Parents are worried about the language and the content their kids might be exposed to when playing these games online, but many parents don't realize that content isn't the only concern.

Online gaming communities are populated with scammers who attempt to prey on young kids. Twitch and Discord, another popular live chat and instant messaging platform made popular during the rise of *Fortnite*, have been criticized for incidents involving cyber predators and sex trafficking. They are also a hotbed for phishing scams. Prominent gamers can solicit donations and paid subscriptions, and there are no parental controls on a site like Twitch.

One vulnerability that makes gamers more susceptible than the average social media user is monetization. Some social media platforms have transactional elements, but this is a common feature of many online games. These elements come in the form of in-game currency that can be used to purchase online perks that enhance the experience. Gamers can also monetize the live streaming of their games to create a more interactive following. It's a way for them to upgrade and personalize the experience they provide, but monetization also creates an avenue of attack for bad actors. Scammers can trick unsuspecting kids into clicking phishing links, scanning fraudulent QR codes, or simply offering up their parents' financial information for these in-game perks. Scammers can use that information to run up fraudulent charges and drain those accounts. But a scam doesn't need to be complicated for it to be effective. Sometimes all scammers need to do is befriend the target.

Kids are trusting, and we've had many customers tell us stories about how their children were duped into trading or handing over their in-game currency for additional perks from their supposed "online friends" that never arrived. There is very little the individual platforms can do in these cases, but the monetary loss is only part of the problem. These experiences can leave children, especially younger kids, feeling humiliated and hurt when they discover they were betrayed by someone online they thought was their friend. It can be an excruciating lesson to learn, but one that can be avoided if you and your kids know what to look out for.

Every family is different, so there is no one-size-fits-all solution for protecting your young gamers but laying down simple ground rules can help ensure your kids are safe online, starting with rules for how they interact on these platforms. It's safest when kids only accept friend requests and participate in private servers with people they already know. Kids can set chat filters to block discrimination, sexually explicit language, hostility, and profanity, but those filters can't block everything. There may be moderators and rules regarding content, but it can be easy to bypass age restrictions for games designed for older players, so you want to pay closer attention to what your kids are doing.

One idea is to keep gaming devices in a common area where you can better see the types of games they play. If you are concerned about a specific game, take some time to familiarize yourself with the content and functionality your kids will encounter. For example, does the game have live chat, video streaming, and in-app purchases? If you're unsure whether a game is age-appropriate, you can check the rating from the Entertainment Software Rating Board (ESRB) or read the reviews on Common Sense Media. And before your child begins playing, familiarize yourself with the game's privacy settings.

Make sure your kids understand the importance of not sharing any personal or financial information online and not clicking any links or scanning any QR codes sent to them. If you choose to make in-game purchases for your kids, only do so on official websites. Don't click on any links that take you to third-party sites.

Whether you're worried about what your kids are doing on social media or if they are vulnerable when gaming online, the best way to protect them is by having open and honest conversations about potential issues. Unfortunately, that is the last thing many parents feel comfortable doing.

## How to Have Those Difficult Conversations with Your Kids

This is where many parents run into a problem because they struggle to talk to their kids about these issues. Eighty-four percent of parents worry that their children aren't safe online, yet they aren't talking to their kids about their concerns.[17] Most parents fear social media affects their teen's ability to socialize, half feel it causes an unhealthy desire for attention and approval, and two-thirds worry their teen is addicted to it.[18] Many parents try to combat this by friending or following their kids on social media, so they can keep tabs on their online behavior. Some even go so far as to create fake accounts, but that can backfire.

According to a Pew Research Center survey of adults with kids ages thirteen to seventeen, 61 percent of parents admitted to checking the websites their children visit.[19] If done properly, that may be beneficial for some families, but it's always best to be open and discuss this with your child, so they don't feel like you're spying on them. Instead, you want them to understand why they should take those added precautions we've discussed. However, that's easier said than done.

Struggling to have these tough conversations isn't necessarily the parents' fault. I get it. For one, it seems like kids speak a different language regarding anything tech or internet related. We're also in a difficult spot because any discussion about this topic could be interpreted by your kids as trying to infringe on their privacy or limit their freedom. That can have adverse effects and make it more likely they hide certain online issues when they arise. But armed with the correct information and an understanding of how your kids are vulnerable on social media can help you better protect them and come to an understanding without conflict. Following this series of steps will help you talk more openly with your kids and earn their trust.

- **Establish rules:** Knowing what you know now, develop a set of fair guidelines regarding device and social media usage. If you follow these rules as well, it will demonstrate that you aren't trying to take away their freedom and will help create a healthier dialogue between you and your kids.

- **Listen:** This shouldn't be a one-sided conversation. Make sure you listen to what your kids say and consider their concerns without judgment. Including them when creating guidelines will make them more likely to adopt these responsible habits.

- **Share information:** Explain why boundaries need to be set. Tell them stories and show them data to help them understand the consequences. This way, they know it's not a punishment. When they better understand how they are vulnerable and what dangers to avoid, they will be more likely to take those precautions independently. They will also be more likely to come to you with a problem. If you're struggling to make your point, consider showing them some popular documentaries. *Screenagers* (for ages ten and up), *The Social Dilemma* (for ages thirteen and up), and *The Great Hack* (for ages fifteen and up) make for excellent and informative viewing.

- **Adapt if necessary:** Every family situation and their online needs are unique. The approach that works well for one family might not be the best for yours. Keep that in mind when talking with your kids and laying out guidelines.

This may be a different world we live in today, but some things never change. Kids will always try to bend the rules, push the limits, and see what they can get away with, just like you did with your parents when you were younger. Any guidelines and guardrails you create will only be as effective as you are at implementing them, so once again, this is a situation where knowledge is power.

If you need help getting started, the Family Online Safety Institute has some excellent resources and sample online safety agreements for teens that you can use to get the ball rolling, but there is no denying that some topics are more difficult to talk about than others. Every situation can be different and requires a different approach. Here is a list of the most common issues parents struggle speaking with their kids about and some information, tools, and resources that you can use to better navigate those conversations and prevent problems before they occur.

## Inappropriate Content

Hackers, scammers, and predators can target your child online, but in some cases, the most damage can be done by their classmates and kids their own age. It starts with the content they share. Almost 50 percent of parents report that their children have been exposed to violent, sexual, or inappropriate content online.[20] That's the last thing any of us want, but with that content only one click away, it seems impossible to prevent.

Parental controls are a simple tool you can use to protect your children without making it feel like you're spying on them. This limits what they can access on all their devices—laptops, desktops, tablets, and phones. It lets you restrict their access to adult content, gaming sites, and content that you feel is inappropriate. You can also filter movies and television shows according to ratings on platforms such as Netflix and Disney+. Certain programs can also help you manage screen time and set guidelines for social media and YouTube usage.

Some platforms, such as Apple's IOS, have features to protect children from viewing (and sending) explicit images. There and warnings and inappropriate photos can be blurred out. Turning on "SafeSearch" on Google Chrome is another simple way to filter out graphic content, and for younger children, while kid-friendly search engines such as KidRex and Kidtopia are excellent options that will show only age-appropriate search results. While these protections can help insulate your children, sometimes they're not enough.[21]

In a time when kids might understand the technological landscape better than you do, a savvy teen has a much better chance of circumventing parental control settings, unlocking devices, or performing a factory reset. So, if you find out that your child came across inappropriate content, try to learn how they got to it. There's a big difference between them getting it from a friend and bypassing the parental controls. Knowing that will determine how best to deal with the situation, and if that content is egregious enough, you can always report it, along with any hate speech or extremist material they encounter.

## Cyberbullying

The more time our children collectively spend online, the more cyberbullying becomes a problem. Since the start of the pandemic, cyberbullying has increased by 40 percent, with 37 percent of kids between twelve and seventeen having suffered from online bullying.[22] Whether they were bullied or not, 90 percent of kids say those in their age range view cyberbullying as a problem.[23]

Bullying occurs in multiple forms. Kids can target another kid directly or can conspire with others to gang up on one individual. One of the most common examples is social exclusion, where kids are deliberately left out of social groups and not invited to various events. Other examples include offensive name-calling, spreading false rumors, receiving unsolicited explicit messages, physical threats, and explicit images of them shared without consent. Social media and gaming platforms are where much of this toxic bullying unfolds.

Cyberbullying can create lasting psychological damage, but many kids choose to suffer in silence. They're embarrassed or feel ashamed, so they don't want to discuss it with anyone. This can make it difficult for you to even know your child is being cyberbullied, but there are offline warning signs that can alert you to potential issues your teens are facing. If your child's grades suffer or they stop being social, that might mean something is up. Changes in sleep and appetite are also often indicative of social troubles. You might even see a change in their digital habits. If they become nervous when online or while receiving texts, there might be a reason for that. Withdrawal from others, low self-esteem, increased anxiety, insecurity, or depression, and overall apathy towards activities they used to enjoy are causes for concern.

It's a difficult conversation to have with your kids, but it's one you can't shy away from. Make sure they understand what type of communication is acceptable online, so they can identify a problem when it occurs. Show them how to document, report, and block any communication with a cyberbully. Let them know they can come to you for help, and if they do, make sure your child feels safe. Listen to them without interrupting and never make excuses for the bully.

If the situation requires you to take action, the G.E.T.R.I.D. method[24] has proven effective, and you can work through the following steps with your child:

- G—Go block or delete the bully on all platforms.
- E—Ensure you keep evidence of bullying.
- T—Tell someone because if your kids talk about it, they can feel less isolated.
- R—Report the abuse to the platform where it occurred.
- I—Initiate control by mitigating without responding or retaliating.
- D—Delete the bullying message after you've taken screenshots as evidence.

If the bully goes to school with your child, report it to the administration because most schools in the United States have anti-bullying policies that cover cyberbullying. Show them any recordings, screenshots, and evidence that provide insight into the frequency and severity of the bullying. If you believe the experience has caused mental or psychological harm, it's worth considering whether your child should see a therapist.

At Aura, we've invested in an intelligent safety start-up called Kidas that has made a promising innovation in cyberbullying prevention technology. Their ProtectMe software, designed specifically to monitor online gaming activity, uses machine learning and other AI to recognize cyberbullying, harassment, racism, hate speech, privacy violations, and any threatening language or behavior that occurs on these platforms. Their research revealed players were exposed to sexual and explicit content and language during one out of every twenty-five conversations. With this software, parents can receive weekly reports that summarize their children's activity while offering personal recommendations if the system detects a situation that needs to be addressed. And it does this while complying with US privacy regulations and without invading your child's own privacy.

While gaming companies and industry associations strive to create more positive and inclusive environments, they remain limited in what they can accomplish. But these intelligent safety innovations can enable protections that go well beyond the manual privacy setting updates and standard content blocking technologies that were once a parent's only option for monitoring their children's gaming content. As more intelligent safety innovations come to market, we'll start to see a paradigm shift in the way parents look to protect their children online.

## Sexting and Sextortion

According to the FBI, in 2021 alone, there were more than 18,000 sextortion-related complaints, but this is deceiving and is probably much higher because kids are less likely to talk to an adult and instead try to block or report the person to the platform. Unfortunately, this isn't very effective, and 50 percent of those who went that route were contacted by the same exact person through a different account or on a completely different platform.[25]

Getting your kids to discuss sexting or sextortion can be uncomfortable, but this is a serious issue. If your child or anyone you know is a victim, you want to follow a similar procedure as cyberbullying by collecting as much evidence as possible. And not only do you want to contact the local police but also the local FBI field office, the FBI's Internet Crime Complaint Center, and possibly even the National Center for Missing and Exploited Children.

Both cyberbullying and sextortion can take an extreme mental toll on kids and teens. They can lead to depression, self-esteem issues, self-harm, and even suicide. This is especially common in sextortion cases because the embarrassment and shame can be so severe.

In 2022, a high school senior in San Jose, California, was sent a nude photo by a scammer posing as a young girl and convinced him to send a nude photo back. As soon as he did, the scammer threatened to send the photo to all of his family and friends if he didn't pay $5,000. He tried to pay some money out of his college fund, but when demands kept increasing, he took his own life.[26]

The troubling increase in sextortion cases and the devastating impact it can have on young kids is just one of many reasons why it's crucial to maintain a healthy dialogue with your children. You want to give them all the tools necessary, so they can navigate these increasingly complicated situations without falling into a trap. And if they do something they might regret, you want them to know they can come to you for help.

Similarly, if you learn that your child is the victim of sextortion or has been targeted by a predator, you immediately want to document everything. Get as much information as possible about the interaction and any details that could help identify that person, such as username, conversations, and time stamps, so you can bring that evidence to law enforcement. In addition to filing a report with the local police department, you also want to file a report with the National Center for Missing and Exploited Children (NCMEC) because they work with the FBI to review the evidence and open investigations. Of course, you can follow their lead and cooperate with investigations, but as soon as you can, your next steps should be to block the predator online so they can't contact your child and then report the incident to the platform.

Social media and the internet should not be a problem when used properly, safely, and in moderation. The problem arises when kids get sucked into the online world to the point where it starts to take over their lives or, worse, begins to replace real-world interactions.

It's not always easy to determine where that line might be, and every child is different, but there are signs when it might be time to have a discussion. If your child is not getting enough physical activity or not getting their schoolwork done, their online behavior might be drifting into unhealthy territory. If you see that your child isn't socializing with friends or family or is not developing proper social skills, that might mean they are spending too much time online. Sleep is another area of concern. Parents might be shocked to learn that a 2022 study revealed that ten-year-old kids lost an average of one night's sleep every week because of social media consumption.[27]

Other more extreme signs might be excessive weight gain, weight loss, or aggressive thoughts, but those could also indicate other issues. Either way, those changes in behavior could be a reason for concern. Any behavioral changes should be taken seriously, whether your child is becoming sexualized too soon, oversharing, not sharing enough, demonstrating an unhealthy need for approval, bullying, or bullying others. It might not be directly linked to their online behavior, but it's worth addressing regardless.

At Aura, we want to help families establish good digital safety habits and get the most out of their online experiences. We also want to help parents set healthy limits, so their lives and their children's lives aren't consumed by those online experiences. In addition to educating yourself on the potential dangers, and implementing the proper protections, having these difficult conversations with your children is often the most effective way you can achieve that goal. However, there is one more thing you want to look out for, and it's a vulnerability that most parents never consider.

## Child Identity Theft

On the surface, it might not seem like your child's identity is all that valuable, but to criminals, it's a blank slate. Minors don't have credit reports, so thieves can use that clean name, Social Security number, date of birth, and identity to personally start over or commit fraud by taking out loans and running up lines of credit.

Technically, it's illegal for anyone under sixteen to apply for loans or credit cards, but few companies verify ages before issuing lines of credit. It's been like this for a while, and it doesn't help that in 2011 the Social Security Administration started issuing randomized Social Security numbers. That made it impossible to determine an applicant's age only by their Social Security number. Most credit card companies have no idea if the applicant is seventy-five years old or a new-born baby.

I know it sounds outrageous, but this type of fraud is on the rise. With the FTC receiving twenty-three thousand reports of identity theft and forty-two thousand reports of fraud for those under nineteen in 2021, the problem will only worsen.[28] And children who frequently use the internet are at a much higher risk of identity theft, which is why so many social media scams specifically target kids by posing as friends or people they trust and try to trick them into giving up their Social Security numbers.

Noah is a current customer who fell victim to identity theft when he was a child but didn't learn about it until he was in his mid-twenties. He went into the family plumbing business right out of high school. Since he did not attend college, he didn't need to take out any loans. He was the type of person who paid for everything in cash—even his first car. He got married in his early twenties to his high school sweetheart, and she was pregnant with their first child when they decided to purchase a home. Much to the couple's surprise, they were denied a loan because of Noah's poor credit, which made no sense to them since he didn't think he had any credit.

They did some digging and learned that someone had taken out a credit card in his name when he was a baby. Given the circumstances, they could easily prove the charges weren't made by Noah, but untangling the legal red tape proved to be a headache that dragged on for ten months. Even during the years after his credit was repaired, his personal information was still used to open up bank accounts and credit cards in his name. He could always get out in front of the issue to prevent any further damage, but those experiences left him on edge and uncertain about the next thing that might happen.

This is not uncommon. A recent Javelin study revealed kids under the age of seven are the most likely victims of child identity theft and fraud.[29] Children are such vulnerable targets for identity theft because the crime can go completely undetected for years. Parents don't think to monitor their children's credit for the simple reason they're kids. It isn't until they are denied a credit card, student loans, or a driver's license or fail a background check that they learn about the fraud. If anything proves that you don't need to be a public figure or have a ton of money in the bank to become a victim of identity theft, it's the fact that children are high-value targets.

In 2020, 1.25 million children in the United States were victims of identity theft. Those numbers were up 25 percent from 2017 when the total number of victims was one million. That means one in fifty children were victims of identity theft. Just to bring this a little closer to home, it's more than likely that one of your kid's classmates (maybe even your own child) will become a victim of identity theft. Cumulative losses from 2020 totaled $918 million.[30] Break those numbers down further, and the fraud cost each affected family more than $1,100 on average.[31]

Armed with only a child's Social Security number, criminals can conduct many of the same types of fraud and identity theft scams they can on adults, and that means many of the warning signs are similar, too. Be on the lookout for bills, credit card offers, calls from collection agencies, notifications from the IRS, or odd junk mail addressed to your child. It's easy to ignore these oddities and assume they are mistakes. While there's a chance that your child might have ended up on a mailing list by accident, unsolicited communications like these are a huge red flag and a potential sign that your child's identity has been stolen. And pay attention if your kids complain about their inability to log into their online accounts because that's an early warning sign as well.

If you believe a scammer has used your child's Social Security number to apply for a credit card, contact the three major credit reporting agencies—Equifax, TransUnion, and Experian—to see if your child already has a credit file in their name. Children under sixteen shouldn't have a credit file, so if they do, it usually means they've been targeted by thieves. If that's the case, ask the bureaus to remove the fraudulent accounts and freeze your child's credit report, so any lenders will have to verify your child's identity before extending credit. Each bureau has slightly different requirements, but they will require proof that you can act on behalf of the minor. Keep track of all the correspondence with these organizations because they will send you a confirmation letter containing your child's credit PIN, which you will need to unfreeze their credit later.

You'll next want to contact any company where your child's identity was used, ask them to close those accounts, and request a letter of confirmation to ensure it was done because sometimes this can fall through the cracks. File an official identity theft report with the Federal Trade Commission and IdentityTheft.gov. You also want to file a police report.

One benefit child victims of identity theft have that adult victims don't is that it may be easier to change their Social Security number, especially if it was used to file fraudulent taxes, government benefits, or employment. If an adult wants to change their Social Security number, they must fit specific strict criteria, but since kids don't have a credit, tax, or employment history, or any other forms of government identification (passport or driver's license), the ripple effects are minimal.

While scammers can get your child's information through malware, hacks, data breaches, physical theft of documents from homes and schools, and tricking victims into offering it up over social media, this type of cybercrime isn't always done by anonymous actors. Seventy percent of child identity theft cases were committed by someone who knew the child, such as a family member or a friend of the family.[32] These individuals often have the easiest access to the minor's sensitive information and can better hide the fraud from the child and the rest of the family.

Financial instability often leads a friend or family member to commit this crime. Not all perpetrators of child identity theft are truly malicious. Some are under such incredible stress and financial hardship that they see opening a line of credit in their child's name as a desperate attempt to get their family out of trouble. They might even fully intend to pay back the debt, but if the situation escalates, all they might do is succeed in setting their child up for their own financial hardships later in life.

When fraud is discovered in these cases, you must follow the same steps to resolve it as any other form of identity theft. You cancel the cards and dispute the fraudulent charges, but while filing a police report isn't always necessary in every case of identity theft, it is a requirement when the fraud is committed by a family member or you know the perpetrator. If you don't, you might be held responsible for the debt, and some institutions require a police report to resolve the fraud.

Worse, withholding information can make you complicit if this person is later accused of committing other crimes.

In identity theft cases like these, many victims don't report the crime to law enforcement and talk very little about it because they don't want to make the family situation any worse. Because of the shame and embarrassment victims of fraud and identity theft can feel, these statistics might be much worse than reported.

It's worth noting that 94 percent of families did not have an identity theft protection service when their child's identity was stolen or their data was leaked. However, three-quarters of those families changed their minds and enrolled in one after the incident.[33] Fortunately, you don't have to learn the hard way.

Antivirus protection and regularly updating the software on all the devices your kids use is an excellent first line of defense against viruses, malware, and ransomware. Even with the proper identity theft protection in place, it's still important to teach your kids about the dangers of not oversharing their personal information online. In an age when kids seem to go through devices faster than they went through baby clothes, make sure you remember to delete all of their personal information (and yours) off their old devices before getting rid of them. Wipe them and restore them to the default factory settings. That's a habit you, as an adult, will also want to get into.

The smaller your child's digital footprint, the better, so you want to limit the number of accounts and services they can sign up for. Think twice about putting their personal information out into the world. When they are old enough to create their own accounts, talk to them about the importance of using strong passwords. And don't ever let your kids enter your credit card or debit card numbers into accounts on their own. To be safest, they shouldn't have access to your financial information at all because some scams try to trick kids into giving it up.

Be especially careful with your child's Social Security number, and keep the physical card in a secure place. The likelihood is that you aren't going to need it, so don't risk misplacing or losing it. Most parents might not realize that the IRS is the only entity that requires your child's Social Security number. Schools and doctors don't need it, but if they insist, ask why, how they'll use it, and how it will be stored. In most cases, you only need to give them the last four digits.

Instead of waiting for identity theft or fraud to occur, you can be proactive. If your children are under sixteen, parents and guardians can freeze their credit. Seventeen- and eighteen-year-olds can freeze their own credit files. Since kids can't legally apply for a credit card until they are sixteen, and you might not want them to have a credit card until they are older anyway, this is a simple preventative step that can save you a lot of headaches. They can then remove the freeze when they are old enough.

If you want to go one step further and build your child's credit, consider piggybacking, which involves adding them as an authorized user on your credit card. I know what you're thinking: *Why would I give my kids a credit card? It's the last thing they need!* That's true, but for this to work, you don't even need to give them the physical card or let them know the account number; just add their name to the account. This allows them to use your good credit to build their own. Some credit card companies have age minimums. For American

Express accounts, authorized users need to be thirteen, and for U.S. Bank, they need to be sixteen, but some credit card companies have no minimum age requirement. With a combination of these proactive financial steps, you can ensure that your child's credit is locked, monitored, and strong, starting from day one.

As a parent, you can't be everywhere. Trying to protect your kids in the real world is hard enough; throw in the potential dangers of the digital world, and it's overwhelming. Just like you wouldn't let your children roam the city alone, you don't want to let them loose on the internet. Luckily, you don't have to.

The internet is an amazing resource, and we want our kids to take advantage of it, but we also want them to be safe. That requires parents to be proactive about their family's digital safety. By helping everyone understand and become more aware of the everyday risks and having the proper protections in place, you can protect every family member from the digital challenges they are guaranteed to experience online.

# CHAPTER 7
# Scammers versus Your Aging Parents

Growing up, we rely on our parents to show us the ropes and teach us right from wrong. Whether helping out with money when we're in a pinch, doling out advice when faced with adversity, or just saying the right thing to pick us up when we're down, we owe our parents a lot. We have the chance to repay that debt as our parents age because the roles begin to reverse, and we suddenly find ourselves the ones who need to look out for them. There is no better example than helping them navigate the ever-changing technological landscape. This goes beyond a simple primer about how to use the devices that have become a staple of the modern world. It now includes protecting them from the scammers who specialize in conning them out of their life savings.

Not only do the elderly have more savings and assets, but senior citizens are also more trusting, which makes them more likely to believe a scammer who claims to be looking out for their best interests. Many elderly victims have trouble remembering details and can easily get confused, especially regarding technology and services they don't understand. That makes them more likely to fall victim to scams over the phone, online, or on social media.

Criminals will often pose as tech support representatives from trusted companies such as Apple or Microsoft who claim their devices are at risk, and they need remote access to fix the issue. Some pretend to be from government agencies, such as the FBI, IRS, or Social Security Administration, to get money, or sometimes just trick them into revealing their personal information. Criminals can dupe the good natured by claiming to be soliciting donations for phony charities, or prey on the hopes of the less fortunate by convincing them they need to pay upfront fees or taxes (or hand over their banking information) to claim money they won in a phony sweepstakes. If your parents are homeowners, they might be targets for reverse mortgage scams designed to trick them out of their money and assets. Many of these scams have been more effective since COVID-19 became rampant; fear and uncertainty makes victims more likely to give out sensitive personal or financial information.

If getting conned out of money wasn't bad enough, there is also the shame that comes with being the victim of a scam. Every victim can feel this, regardless of age, but seniors may worry that reporting the fraud or telling family members could limit their freedom, so they don't seek help. This can make the problem worse and the destruction more devastating, but in many of these cases, the target isn't the only victim. This type of crime has ripple effects that can reverberate throughout the family, putting added stress and financial burden on loved ones, which makes it so important that you and your aging parents know what to look out for and how to protect yourself.

Robocalls, phishing messages, and spam emails are not reserved for the elderly, but scams are more effective with this demographic because these attacks were designed to exploit vulnerable and trusting targets. Cybercriminals target vulnerabilities, and as we age, one of the most significant vulnerabilities is our increasing dependence on health care.

## Medical and Medicare Scams

In 2022, two women working with a Colombian national living in Florida and his network of associates conned Medicare out of $107 million![1]

This criminal organization used the Medicare data they had purchased from foreign and domestic call centers that targeted senior citizens. They went so far as to get call center representatives to offer those on Medicare access to what is known as durable medical equipment, which includes expensive back and shoulder braces. They then submitted those phony claims to Medicare, but it was all done without any prescription or documentation that this equipment was needed. Not only were the claims fraudulent, but they submitted multiple claims for some patients, and even submitted claims for patients that were dead. Sometimes the equipment never arrived, and sometimes they billed Medicare twelve times the actual price of the equipment. They made so much money that they established shell companies made to look like medical equipment providers in twelve different states to process the payments.[2]

To avoid detection, they fielded all of the phone calls from patients complaining they received equipment they didn't need. They also tried to fend off the insurance company who kept asking about medical records and prescription orders, but they were eventually caught. The two women each pleaded guilty to one count of conspiracy to commit health fraud. They were sentenced to three years of supervised release, and barred from doing business in the healthcare industry. It might sound like they got off easy, but one was forced to pay $8.6 million in restitution and the other $20.7 million.

Medical identity theft comes in many different forms but primarily involves scammers using the victim's health insurance information to gain illegal access to medical services, equipment, prescription drugs, or to be reimbursed for fraudulent claims. These scams are incredibly lucrative, and almost two-thirds of victims report losing more than $13,500 to fraudulent billing.[3] Health care information is extremely valuable and, according to the dark web price index, can cost up to $1,000. That's two hundred times the value of credit card information and one thousand times the value of a stolen Social Security card.

Thieves commit medical identity theft for the same reason they target children: because it can take a very long time for the victims to discover the crime. That means they can steal more money over an extended period. After all, you can't get caught when the victims don't even know a crime has been committed. Many people don't realize they have been targeted until they visit the doctor or require an emergency procedure. By that time, the victim may be on the hook for thousands and thousands of dollars. That's why the potential losses are so high.

What makes these scams so insidious is that medical identity theft comes with the additional burden of wreaking havoc on your health care coverage, which can leave you without a safety net when you need it most. Even once the crime has been discovered, it can take the authorities and insurance companies a long time to sort out the fraud, which can lead to delays in getting essential medical care. Those consequences can be dire.

Because there is so little oversight in the Medicare system, it's widely susceptible to fraud and has become difficult to properly monitor. Even doctors can become victims. Sixty-eight-year-old Louisiana physician Pamela Ganji was wrongfully convicted of conspiracy to commit Medicare fraud and sentenced to six years in prison. She served several months before the appellate court reversed the decision.[4]

Medicare fraud and medical identity theft scams are carried out the same way as other forms of identity theft. It all starts with data, and protected healthcare information is the second most common type of information hacked in data breaches. In 2021 alone, 45 million people had their personal healthcare information exposed during healthcare cyberattacks.[5] Many of these data breaches expose millions of patients' information, which is used to conduct various scams. Here are some of the most common to be on the lookout for:

- **New medicare cards:** Scammers will phone the victim to say Medicare is issuing new cards, and their current card is invalid. To get the new card, scammers ask the victim to provide their personal information over the phone. Some scammers may try to alleviate any concern by assuring the victim that they aren't asking for their Social Security number or bank account information, only their Medicare number. However, that

Medicare number is what they're really after because it's extremely valuable.

- **Inactive medicare account:** This is a similar scam where criminals call the victim and convince them to reveal their personal information to keep their Medicare account active. Some scammers create a sense of urgency by threatening to cancel the account if they don't provide the information.

- **Free medical supplies and services:** This is the perfect example of how your data can be used against you. If scammers can learn about your medical conditions, they can target you by making specific offers, such as a discount on diabetes testing supplies. They will then try to get your Medicare number and maybe even a credit card number they say they need for shipping costs. Similar scams lure potential victims by claiming they are eligible for genetic testing that can help identify cancer, heart disease, and other conditions. They may claim that the services are free as a ruse to get that Medicare number. They might also promise to send free at-home tests.

- **Refunds:** Who doesn't like hearing they have been overcharged and are owed money? That's why so many unsuspecting senior citizens fall for this scam when someone claiming to be from the Medicare office calls and says they are owed hundreds of dollars. This gets victims to put their guard down and offer their personal and financial information to facilitate this phony refund. Urgency is created when scammers tell the victim they must act now, or they might lose out on the refund.

- **Preapproval for a better plan:** This one is common during open enrollment periods and targets those weighing their coverage options or signing up for Medicare for the first time. Health care is the subject of massive confusion, and with high costs, everyone looks for ways to save money and avoid paying for services they don't need. The problem is that understanding all the ins and outs of the Medicare system is no easy task. That's what criminals prey on. They will often call, claiming that the victim has been pre-approved for a Medicare Advantage plan with more benefits. The problem is that Medicare Advantage is not affiliated with the federal government. Most people don't know that, which is why these scams can be so effective.

There are two simple ways to weed out potential Medicare scams.

First, if you are enrolled in Medicare, your Medicare number is on file and the organization will never call the customer to ask for their Medicare number or for any financial information.

Second, you will rarely ever get a phone call from Medicare. In fact, there are only two reasons why Medicare would call you. First, a Medicare health or drug plan provider (or the agent who enrolled you in the plan) may contact you if you are already a member of the program if there is an issue with your account. Second, a customer service representative may call you if you left them a message or if Medicare sent you a letter saying they will contact you. So, if you receive a call from someone claiming to be associated with Medicare, hang up and call Medicare back directly at 1-800-MEDICARE or contact their fraud hotline at 1-800-HHS-TIPS.[6]

It's important to understand that it's not only scammers committing this fraud. Insider fraud occurs when someone working in the medical system, including the Department of Health and Human Services, uses or sells the patient's information to scammers. This can be highly lucrative for criminals. Dr. Lilit Gagikovna Baltaian was arrested on criminal healthcare fraud charges for falsely certifying patients to receive home health care. Over six years, she billed Medicare for expenses that totaled $6,029,674. She is currently facing ten years in prison.[7]

Similar to the fraud committed against children, six out of ten cases of elder abuse are committed by people the victim knows, specifically friends, family members, and children.[8] On average, they steal $116,000 from their victims.[9] They may trick them into signing over access to their assets and financial accounts or convince them to sign over their power of attorney.

To help insulate your aging parents against these vicious Medicare scams, make sure they keep their health insurance and Medicare cards secure. They should treat these cards like they would a Social Security card and immediately contact the insurance company if they are lost. They shouldn't share this or any healthcare information, including login and portal credentials, with anyone. It's a good idea to opt for paperless bills to reduce the chance this information can be stolen from the mail. Whenever a bill arrives, examine the charges to make sure that everything listed was related to your medical care. Don't ever ignore mistakes on bills, calls about medical debt, or insurance claims being denied. It's easy for you or your parents to assume that it will all sort itself out if you didn't do anything wrong. That can be a costly mistake that leads to a lot of headaches.

If you learn your parents are a victim of medical identity theft, you want to act immediately by filing a police report with local law enforcement and a report at IdentityTheft. gov. Document the fraud as accurately as possible and ask for copies of records from all medical and insurance providers because the FTC will start an investigation and create a recovery plan. However, don't solely rely on them. Send a written letter to the healthcare provider explaining the situation and requesting that the records be amended. In these instances, the provider must respond in thirty days. Check credit reports to see if there are any additional instances of fraud, and freeze your credit if necessary. At the very least, set up a fraud alert.

Senior citizens see more doctors and have more medical bills, which makes them ideal victims of healthcare scams. Add in all the confusion surrounding insurance, Medicare, and the system in general, and it's a recipe for disaster if you don't know what to look for. However, there is another major vulnerability of the elderly that scammers have learned to exploit, and it's one that often flies under the radar, making it that much more effective. That vulnerability is loneliness.

## Preying on Loneliness

While online dating and dating apps are common among the younger generation, they are also gaining popularity among the elderly. Lonely and trusting seniors can be seduced when given attention and affection by a scammer. Skilled con artists can research their targets and use any information gathered online or through social media to build trust. And once they have that trust, they can request money. They often concoct elaborate stories of how they need money for unexpected medical expenses and other emergencies. It may seem like an obvious scam to an outsider, but when someone's emotions have been manipulated, it's much more challenging to see the ruse for what it is because you so desperately want what they're saying to be true.

While these scams may not be as common as other scams that target seniors, they result in the most significant losses.[10] In 2020, one scammer stole the identity of a Florida woman and posed as that woman on a dating service where she befriended an eighty-year-old widower. This was a long con, and the scammer created a backstory about being in the art world and owning a gallery. She (I say "she," but the scammer could have been a man; we don't know because the person was never caught) seduced the victim and then built trust before asking for help with a venture. The scammer claimed she needed to raise $5 million to ship a five-hundred-ton marble sculpture from China and promised to pay back any investment and a percentage of the profits. Along with the detailed backstory, the scammer also made fraudulent documents and contracts. Over five months, she stole more than $200,000. The money was sent to different overseas accounts. Investigators searched but had no luck recovering the money or learning the scammer's identity.[11]

Scammers who prey on the elderly using romance scams fall into a predictable pattern, but the most effective ones are charming and seductive, so the con often goes undetected. Most will always have an excuse not to meet in person or over video chat because they don't want to be identified. One way they avoid that is by claiming to be active service members stationed overseas. The pictures they post online are typically taken from other profiles, and once they've seduced their victim, they ask for financial help. They sometimes even ask for money so they can travel to meet their victim in person. Similar to the story above, many of these scams are centered around a false investment or investment opportunities that turn out to be cons.

If your parent lives alone and has joined a dating site to meet people, you want to make sure they know the warning signs of a romance scam. It's also important to understand that these scams aren't reserved only for dating apps. Con artists can prey on victims using social media sites as well. Some of these long cons can start with a simple Facebook message.

Dating and romantic relationships aren't the only way that the elderly try to combat loneliness. Many seek companionship from friends and family and will often jump at the chance to spend more time with their grandkids. Scammers know this and use it to their advantage.

Barbara was an eighty-year-old widow. She lived in a retirement community only a few miles away from her son and his family. She would visit on holidays, but once her two grandsons got to high school, they didn't visit as much as they used to. She would have liked to see more of them, but she also knew they had their own lives, so she didn't push the issue. That's why when she saw her grandson Matt calling her cellphone one afternoon, she perked up, but quickly grew concerned when he said he was calling from a hospital in Canada. He broke his leg and received treatment, but they wouldn't release him until he paid the $10,000 bill. He asked if she could send him the money via Zelle and begged her not to tell his parents because he would get in trouble. Barbara was concerned and glad to help. She followed the instructions and sent the money. She even kept her word by not telling his parents. The problem was that Matt wasn't in a hospital in Canada. He wasn't in any trouble at all because it wasn't Matt who called her.

This is referred to as the grandparents' scam, and there are different ways it can unfold, but it typically involves the scammer posing as a grandchild in trouble, asking for a large payment to be sent, and then swearing the victim to secrecy.

What makes some scammers so convincing is that they've done their research. Given all the information that can be gleaned online and over social media, they're able to know the grandchildren's names and can then pepper in those authentic details. This way, elderly victims don't think twice. Savvy scammers can spoof the grandchild's phone number, so the victim has much less reason to doubt the story. The reason they swear the grandparent to secrecy is because it makes the victim feel like a trusted confidant and delays the identification of the scam. Combine this with the looming threat and urgency created over the phone, and victims are caught off guard, making it less likely they will do their due diligence to verify these claims. When it comes time to collect, scammers either ask that the money be wired, or can send ride-sharing services to pick up the cash, and the victims never hear from them again.

The best protection against this scam is to make sure your parents know to never send anyone money without verifying the information first. The MO of these scammers is to ask for cash, gift cards, and wire transfers while using emotional language and insisting victims act fast without looking into these claims. Unsolicited calls that fit these criteria are always a scam. Knowing that in advance makes it less likely the victim will be fooled. And, when in doubt, contact the local police department directly before taking further action.

This is a scam that any trusting grandparent can easily fall for, but some of the most vulnerable targets are those who have just lost their partner. Unfortunately, that's a very real scenario you'll have to deal with at some point, and you want to ensure that your family isn't being taken advantage of during the grieving process.

## Defrauding the Deceased

Losing a loved one can be heartbreaking. Making arrangements and filing all the necessary paperwork can be especially difficult during those times. It would be nice to think the dead were off-limits to cybercriminals, but sadly they aren't. Credit bureaus and government agencies can take weeks to register someone as deceased. That creates a window of opportunity thieves try to exploit.

Information is power for any cybercriminal. Some scammers follow the obituary pages to look for targets. If they can learn the deceased's address, they can file a change of address form with the post office shortly after their victim has passed away. They then place a three-day hold on the mail, so any living relatives won't receive notification about the change of address. During that very short window, thieves can open up lines of credit in the deceased's name and run up massive charges. Just like credit card companies have very little oversight to determine if an applicant is a grown adult or a newborn baby, they don't have the ability to distinguish the living from the dead either.

Stealing someone's identity after they pass away is referred to as ghosting, and there are a few different ways this can unfold. Despite the different methods, they all take advantage of the sensitive nature of the event to trick loved ones when their guard is down. One common way they do that is through the promise of financial assistance.

These are particularly cruel scams, but there are ways to protect your family from being victimized when they are grieving the loss of a loved one. Here are a few simple steps:

- Don't include any sensitive information in the obituary. That includes birthday, birthplace, address, middle name, and mother's maiden name because those are often the standard answers to many password-recovery questions. It's also best to avoid mentioning family members to prevent them from being targeted by criminals.
- Obtain copies of the death certificate. This may seem like a formality at first, but once the death is officially recorded, that certificate will help prevent you and your family from being on the hook for fraudulent charges.
- Alert any one of the three major credit bureaus about the death. A "deceased" notice on their report serves as a permanent credit freeze that prevents anyone from stealing their identity and opening fraudulent lines of credit in their name.
- Identify any outstanding debts. Get out in front of scammers by learning about the deceased's financial

situation. This will prevent you from any unexpected surprises down the road.

- Notify all the financial institutions where the deceased had accounts, including banks and credit card companies. Anyone who tries to use their identity after this will raise a red flag.
- Contact all the insurance companies where the deceased had policies, including home, auto, mortgage, and life. This will prevent scammers from applying for a reverse mortgage in the deceased's name.
- Alert the IRS and file any remaining tax returns. To prevent the identity theft of a deceased person, the IRS requires you to send a death certificate along with the last tax return. Eligible survivors can then claim the decedent's refund.
- Contact the Social Security Administration and provide them with a death certificate. A funeral home might do this, but it's always best to follow up to ensure the SSA has everything they need.
- Contact the DMV because, depending on the state where you live, you might have to cancel the driver's license of the deceased yourself, either in person or by mail. This will go far in preventing identity theft as the driver's license is a crucial piece of information used by scammers.

I know that's a lot, and it can make an already difficult time even harder, but it's necessary if you want to prevent fraud. While identity theft protection can take a lot of pressure off, you still want to tie up loose ends.

## How to Protect Your Parents

The most important thing you can do to protect your parents from scammers is to have an open and honest conversation. Every family situation is different, so you know how best to approach your parents about specific issues.

No matter what your family dynamic looks like, you want to understand and sympathize with the challenges they now encounter. We all lead busy lives but keeping in regular contact and frequently checking in with your parents to better understand what's going on in their lives is a simple way to strengthen your relationship and combat any potential loneliness. You can always offer to lend a helping hand when it comes to looking over their medical statements or making sure they come to you first with any tech support issues before trying to navigate that complex world on their own. You also want to avoid judgment and keep the lines of communication open. That's crucial in getting your parents to come to you if they experience any suspicious activity. Make sure they understand that anybody can get scammed, and people of all ages fall victim to fraud. Show them the statistics and tell them what to look out for.

Their first line of defense is being suspicious of any unsolicited calls or messages. Companies such as Apple and Microsoft will never call them about issues with their devices. And no website can tell them their device has been infected with viruses. All the unsolicited calls, emails, and pop-ups with promises to clean up their computer and speed up their devices are scams. The same is true about agencies like the FBI, IRS, or Social Security Administration. Representatives from these agencies will rarely reach out, so if you or your parents receive unsolicited calls from someone claiming to be a tech support or government to representative, it's almost always a scam. If ever in doubt, hang up, and call the agency back at their official number.

Make sure your parents know not to ever send money, download files, or click links without doing due diligence. And if an investment opportunity sounds too good to be true, it probably is. So, anyone claiming to provide high returns with little risk and guaranteeing a profit, doesn't have your parents' best interest in mind. To avoid your parents being manipulated in a grandparent's scam, consider creating a secret family password that any member can use over the phone or in texts and emails to let each other know that the transaction is real and not a scam.

It might seem like identifying these elder scams should be easy, but it can be challenging for them to remain calm and make the proper decision at the moment, especially if approached with the possible danger of a family member. Skilled scammers know how to manipulate, and the best can be incredibly convincing. They talk quickly, create a sense of urgency, and then force victims to make snap decisions by claiming they need to act fast. If you believe this will be a problem for your parents, create notes and keep them by the phone or computer with a series of steps to follow if they find themselves in a suspicious situation. Here's a standard protocol that's worked for some of our customers:

- **Stop:** Take the time to breathe and think. Once calm, take note of any suspicious behaviors or requests. If someone is pressing for an answer, they are probably a scammer.

- **Leave:** If the caller or emailer does raise red flags, hang up or close out the email.
- **Ask:** Call a trusted family member to explain the situation and begin searching for more information to see if what the caller claimed was legitimate.
- **Wait:** Don't act. Don't click any links. And don't send any money. Sit with what you've learned and take the time to develop a plan.
- **Act:** Call verified phone numbers and visit official websites to determine if the request is legitimate.

Always err on the side of caution, because a little bit of suspicion can save you a ton of trouble. As with any form of identity theft, prevention is the best defense. Knowing what to look out for, and being able to quickly identify a scammer's strategy, will make life easier for you and your parents. However, we all make mistakes when it comes to digital safety. We click links we shouldn't, give out information we should keep private, and don't always practice proper digital safety habits. It's hard enough for each of us to follow all of these steps on our own, never mind getting children, family members, and aging parents to all do the same. That's where intelligent safety can be your extra set of eyes, monitoring all the nooks and crannies where scammers can wreak havoc.

# CHAPTER 8

# Protecting Your Family Finances

Adam was a sixty-year-old contractor who had been in construction for most of his life. He worked hard to build his business and had started the process of handing over the reins to his two sons as he prepared for retirement. When he received a call from a Bank of America representative telling him that his savings account had been compromised, he wanted to do everything possible to protect the $50,000 he had in that account.

The representative on the other end of the line was polite, offering to help, and the caller ID on the phone indicated the call was from Bank of America, so Adam believed the rep when he said someone from another state was trying to make a large withdrawal, and he needed to act fast to prevent fraud. According to the rep, the best way to protect his money was to move it to another bank. The rep walked him through the process of using Zelle to transfer half of the money from a savings account to a Chase account. While making the transfer, there was a voice in Adam's head telling him that something was off, but he ignored that gut instinct and hit send.

That voice only got louder once he hung up the phone, and once Adam couldn't find any record of the money in a new account, he realized that he had been conned. He immediately phoned Bank of America who confirmed that no representative phoned him about a problem with his account. They said they would look into the matter, but since Adam initiated the transfer of funds, the bank was limited in what it could do to recover the money. In these situations, it's not their responsibility; the onus is on the individual, so Adam hired a forensic accounting specialist to try and track down his money.

What makes this crime so difficult to solve is that when criminal organizations con a victim into transferring their money into a separate account, the criminals immediately transfer it elsewhere. That makes it incredibly difficult for even the most competent detective teams to return the stolen money and bring the scammer to justice. It's been six months, and Adam has come to terms with the fact that his money is most likely gone.

Social engineering attacks like these are so common and highly effective. And they can take on many forms. Steven D. Short and Karissa L. Dyar started cold-calling people with credit card debt, claiming they could reduce their interest rates and save them thousands. All people had to do was pay upfront fees that ranged between $695 and $1,495. They even promised to refund the money if interest rates weren't reduced. They created phony businesses and used them to steal more than $11 million from thousands of people before being caught by the FTC.[1]

To pull off these interest-rate-reduction scams, thieves pose as representatives from well-known lenders to lure victims with promises of being able to lessen the burden. When you're in debt and struggling to keep up with payments, it's easy to believe people who tell you what you want to hear.

Fraudsters keep a pulse on the issues stressing the American family. They are very knowledgeable about the benefits that Americans have access to, particularly government benefits, so these criminals target Americans with access to those funds. That's why our veterans and active-duty military members have been an increasing target for financial fraud. According to a 2022 survey by Ipsos, 71 percent of veterans and active-duty service members reported being a victim of digital crime compared to only 60 percent of the total population.[2]

In 2021, the military community reported more than 200,000 instances of fraud, identity theft, and scams that cost their families more than $267 million. One in six of those veterans and service members who fell victim to digital crime experienced financial loss, and one in ten will not be able to resolve the issue.[3] One of the most popular scams target their military pensions. Criminals try to get upfront payments for the promise of bigger returns (or secret government funding for programs that don't exist) only to steal their money and their benefits.

Financial fraud has existed as long as there has been money. It evolves over time, and as our lives shift more online and more goods and services are available with the simple click of a button, we've all become bigger targets because that convenience exposes a new vulnerability. That means everyone is at risk today. No group is safe because it doesn't matter how much money you have in the bank to become a target.

# How to Protect Yourself When Shopping Online

Think about the time you save by shopping online. When you realize you need something or have to buy a last-minute gift, you can find what you need in a few minutes. That beats getting in the car, driving to the store, and walking up and down the aisles. And the internet never closes. It's incredibly convenient, which is why online shopping scams and the nondelivery of goods purchased were the second most common internet crime in 2021, with $337 million lost.[4]

We've become so used to instantly paying for anything we want that it's easy to be careless with our financial information. Unlike your Social Security number, your credit card number is much harder to protect because you need to expose that information to use it. I'm not advocating that you cut up your credit cards and revert back to cash. However, there are precautions you can put in place to protect yourself and your family. It comes down to a four-pronged approach that includes digital habits, payment methods, shipping, and real-world protections.

## #1. Digital Habits

The first thing you want to do before purchasing or paying for anything online is make sure the website is legitimate.

It's best to stick with the major retailers whenever possible. Amazon, Target, Best Buy, and Walmart invest in creating a safe online shopping experience. However, some scammers take advantage of this by creating fake websites; some are even designed to look like these major retailers.

Fake online stores can be a significant source of revenue for criminals. They get you to put in your credit card details for a product that never arrives, or you might receive a different product entirely. The benefit of sending the wrong product is that it's much more challenging to refute the charge and get your money back when there is a record of a product being delivered. Meanwhile, they get what they're really after: your credit card information.

Anyone can create a website with a hacked account using stock photos and fake reviews. They can post fake ads on social media to direct traffic. Forty percent of these shopping scams originated with an ad on Instagram or Facebook.[5] Social media ads and unsolicited emails lure you to these unsecured online stores. They try to make it look like you've shopped there before, but email messages embedded in an image, misspellings, and senders whose email address doesn't match the company are all dead giveaways that the online store is not legitimate. However, don't assume stores that appear in a Google search are automatically legitimate either because almost 50 percent of victims of this fraud arrived at the phony site through a Google search.[6] So, how do you know if a site is legitimate?

First, look for HTTPS (not HTTP) and the padlock symbol in the address bar. If the SSL (secure sockets layer) is valid, the symbol will be locked. If a site doesn't have these protections, don't proceed. Even if the site is legitimate, it can be a target for hackers. Unsecure websites are a red flag, but they aren't the only red flag. Eighty-three percent of scam and phishing sites used HTTPS, and 94 percent had a valid SSL.[7]

You can identify these scams in other ways, and many telltale signs are in the look and design of the site. Low-quality images, generic photos, spelling mistakes, grammatical errors, improper English, and just a poor overall appearance are signs. Snoop around these phony websites long enough, and you will often find other anomalies, such as reviews that don't match the products or no "about us" page, so you can't find any information on the store.

Scammers hope that shoppers won't look closely enough to notice, and they try to distract them with discount luxury goods and bargain pricing that seem too good to be true. That often gets people's attention. However, it's not just phony or nonexistent products these scammers are hocking. The purpose of some of these scams might be to get you to click links, so they can download malware on your computer. If ever in doubt, a simple Google search can reveal a lot, and you can always check to see if the store is listed on BBB's scam tracker website.

## #2. Payment Methods

Once you've determined that a site is legitimate and it comes time to pay, always choose credit over debit. Always!

You have a safety net when using your credit card, one there is a very good chance that you've already taken advantage of at some point. Credit card liability policies protect you, so you aren't on the hook for fraudulent charges. If you report the fraud within sixty days, under the Fair Credit Billing Act, you're liable for only $50, but some major credit card companies, such as Visa, Mastercard, Discover, and American Express, offer $0 fraud liability. That's security you aren't guaranteed with debit cards.

If you use your debit card and the site turns out to be a scam, not only is it more difficult to be reimbursed for that money, but thieves now also have access to your bank credentials. That can create a much bigger headache. Peter Dolce learned this the hard way when one scammer used his bank account number and debit card information to slowly siphon $13,000 out of his account over several months. And since he didn't discover and report some of these fraudulent transactions in enough time, his bank wouldn't issue a refund.[8]

Credit may be the preferred payment method online, but make sure you don't store your credit card with an online store. I know this is a hard one because it's so convenient and makes things much easier, but by creating a guest account and entering your card manually each time, you protect your financial information from being scooped up in data breaches. If you must create a profile, provide as little personal and financial information as possible. This is particularly important with smaller retailers who have less security because the financial information they keep on file for their customers can more easily be captured by determined hackers. Still, big companies get hacked, too. It happens all the time.

If you need to use an alternative method, opt for PayPal because those who used it on fraudulent websites lost significantly less money than those who used Cash App, Zelle, Venmo, Apple Pay, or made any wire transfers. It's difficult to recoup any losses with Zelle in particular, and it's reported less than 1 percent of victims were able to get their money back.[9]

When it comes to sites like Facebook Marketplace or other public forums, scams can work both ways, and sellers are also at risk. Phony buyers can pay for items using stolen credit cards, which leaves the seller on the hook if the transaction is later reversed. That's why it's always recommended to only accept payments from PayPal or Facebook Checkout, and not

Cash App, Venmo, or wire transfers. Some fake buyers over-pay and then ask for a refund, claiming it was a mistake. But since the credit cards are stolen or payment methods fraudulent, sellers are on the hook.

## #3. Shipping

When shopping online, shipping is another potential vulnerability to look into before pulling the trigger on any order. Some shady retailers might tack on exorbitant shipping fees. That's one reason the price of luxury items might seem too good to be true.

Fake shipping notifications with updates and reports on delays can buy the scammers time before the fraud is reported. This lets them scam more people before they close up shop and disappear without a trace. So, if you experience delays, check the shipping confirmation. Also, check the tracking number with the shipping site's official page, whether it's the U.S. Postal Service, UPS, or FedEx. If it doesn't show up on those sites, there's a good chance it's a scam.

If you're a seller, don't be fooled if buyers ask to send you prepaid shipping labels. They may claim to have a preferred shipping method and offer to pay for it, but this allows them to change the package's destination. They can then claim the package never arrived, and since you don't have the tracking information, there is no way to prove they received it.

## #4. Real-World Protections

You can be extremely careful with how you shop online and do everything we've discussed right, but none of that matters if you're using compromised public Wi-Fi. Hackers can exploit unprotected networks to intercept your connection, access your devices, and collect any payment or financial information you share when on that network. Some go so far as to create phony Wi-Fi signals or hotspots that coax people into submitting their credit card information before gaining access.

What happens if you click a suspicious link containing malware and haven't updated your devices or antivirus software? A simple mistake like that could give criminals access to your credit card information. Failing to practice good digital safety habits and protect your devices can make all the other protections you have in place irrelevant. Everything works together because it only requires one vulnerability during one moment for your information to be exposed. That's why a VPN and antivirus software are so valuable, but even then, you want to be careful with your financial information when out in public.

You have no idea who might be shoulder surfing and watching your screen for financial and login information. If you do a lot of shopping when out and about, take advantage of retailer mobile apps. These can be a much safer alternative than making purchases over their website. Just make sure they are updated because they can be hacked, too.

Real-world protections begin with device security and include your real-world behavior. You can't be so focused on preventing online fraud that you forget to protect your financial information in the real world. How do you use your physical card? How many cards do you have? Do you carry all of them with you or just the ones you need? Do you use a chip reader, or do you swipe? Have you ever given anyone your credit card or banking information over the phone? What do you do with credit card bills or any statements that contain your financial information? Protecting your real-world financial information is essential to insulate you against fraud.

The reality is that financial fraud isn't going anywhere. This will remain a problem as long as money is transferred digitally. Sure, there are some added protections that financial institutions can put into place to further insulate you and protect your money, but given what we've seen so far, it's unlikely that people will trade convenience for security. A culture that has become so used to buying whatever we want with one click might not accept a more thorough checkout process, even if it does offer more security. While you can't prevent all fraud from ever occurring, you can significantly limit the chance of it happening to you. It starts by having the right protections in place, but often the best way to insulate yourself and your family are the steps you personally take every day.

# CHAPTER 9

# Nurturing Healthy Digital Safety Habits

There is no one way to stop cybercrime. A scam that begins on Instagram could result in credit fraud. A phishing link sent in a text message that you accidentally click on could result in your bank account being drained. Any one attack can evolve and unfold in different areas of the digital landscape—that's the reason why comprehensive and interconnected solutions are so important. However, when looking to prevent any of these dramatically different cyberattacks, the answers often trace back to the same fundamental behaviors and actions that comprise good digital safety habits.

Whether safeguarding your online banking app, securing your child's Instagram account, or making sure your aging parents don't send their money to someone claiming to be from the IRS, there are tried and true preemptive actions that will significantly reduce your risk of falling victim to identity theft or fraud.

The threat of cybercrime can feel overwhelming. If I didn't know it before, I was definitely reminded of it after compiling all the information required for this book. Nobody can be expected to keep track of everything; I know I can't. That's why I've created this cheat sheet that contains the most critical elements that make up good digital safety habits. Some of these you might already practice, but this chapter is meant to be both a reference and a reminder of the healthy habits you want to practice and instill in your family members.

## Passwords

Let's begin with the first and often best line of defense.

Passwords are the most basic but essential security feature protecting any account. They are the equivalent of locking your front door, yet so many people mess this up. Even when the dangers of reusing the same password and creating weak passwords are explicitly explained, people still do it! And if you think your passwords are weak, imagine how unsecure your kids' passwords are. Until going password-less becomes universal, we're stuck with passwords, and it's in your best interest to make sure they're strong and unique.

When selecting a password, there are some clear ground rules. The first is don't use "123456*." That was the most popular password leaked in 2019 and 2020. "Password" was number three on that list in both years.[1] Avoid using easy-to-find data or personal details, like your pet's name, anniversary, birthday, or phone number.

Password hacking software checks for commonly used phrases, numbers, and adjacent keyboard combinations in less than a second. Just for a frame of reference, an eight-character password with only lowercase letters can be hacked instantly. Throw in one uppercase letter, and that timeframe jumps to twenty-two minutes. Add a number, and it goes up to an hour. Place a symbol in there, and it's eight hours. But if you have a twelve-character password with at least one uppercase letter, number, and symbol, it will take that same computer 34,000 years.[2]

Now, you can understand why your online accounts constantly ask you to update your password using these criteria. Here are some simple ground rules you can follow when creating passwords.

- A long password is a strong password. You want to shoot for at least twelve characters. Sixteen is better. Why? Every extra character makes that password significantly harder to hack by adding an additional layer of protection. One tip is to consider pass-phrases that are easy for you to remember, but difficult for anyone else to predict. Something like, "Ionlyeatcoconutsinmay."
- Make it random. Don't pick a word, name, date, or phrase you have any connection with.
- Never reuse passwords, even if the account is old or you don't use it anymore. Those MySpace login credentials from fifteen years ago can wind up on the dark web, and if that password matches any of your current accounts, hackers can gain access. This was how Mark Zuckerberg got hacked, so it's probably more common than you realize.
- Have it generated! Save yourself the time and the headache of having to come up with a password, and just let a password generator do it for you.
- Use a password manager. This saves you from keeping track of dozens of unique passwords. It does everything for you, and all you need to do is remember one password.

Consider it a good thing if you can't remember your passwords. If you don't know your passwords and follow these simple steps, the odds of your accounts being hacked shrink considerably.

Customers always ask us, "What happens if hackers break into the password manager and then have access to the login credentials of all my accounts?" It's good that you're thinking that way, but password managers are encrypted, and it would take more computation than is readily available on earth to crack that encryption. You should be all set with that level of protection.

All of these rules also apply to PINs. If thieves ever get ahold of your debit card, the first thing they will try are birthdays, phone numbers, and addresses. PINs can be especially vulnerable because savvy pickpockets can watch you type in the PIN at an ATM or in a grocery checkout line before lifting your wallet, so be extra careful in public. And you never want to write down or keep passwords and PINs in your wallet. That's just making things too easy for hackers.

After going through all this trouble to keep your passwords safe, you don't want to slip up and make the mistake of giving them out over the phone, text, or email. This is true even if you're using a more secure messaging app like Telegram. And don't store your passwords (or any important personal or financial information, for that matter) on your devices. That means don't keep passwords in the Notes on your iPhone. If it's hacked, you've essentially handed thieves the key to every account you have.

## Multifactor Authentication

Multifactor authentication takes the password to the next level and provides an additional layer of security. Most major financial and social media accounts use this feature, so it's one you're probably familiar with. But since there is an extra step involved, it's a safety measure that many people bypass. Do so at your own peril.

Frequently called two-factor authentication, it involves putting in a one-time code in addition to your password. That code is often sent via text message when you try to sign in. It's only valid for a short period, usually only a few minutes, so it's incredibly secure. The true benefit of multifactor authentication is that you don't only need the password to log into an account, but you also need the right device, which is often a phone.

Nothing is entirely foolproof, and there are scams, like the SIM swap Lauren succumbed to in the opening chapter, that can bypass multifactor authentication. In that case, hackers had access to her phone, so they received the sign-in code. If you want an extra layer of protection beyond a code being sent via text, try an authenticator app, such as Google Authenticator or Microsoft Authenticator. And avoid single-account sign-in options that allow you to sign into other accounts with existing accounts, such as Google, Apple, or Facebook. This is basically like using the same password for each account. Some Google login buttons on popular job portals appear to be a convenient way to upload your resume, but end up providing the site access to all of your digital files.[3]

In October 2022, Meta published a report, revealing how they discovered more than four hundred malicious apps specifically designed to get users' Facebook credentials by encouraging them to sign-in with Facebook after download-ing.[4] No matter how much these companies try to prevent fraud and are on the lookout for these malicious apps, they're not going to catch everything.

## Browsing Options

How do you feel knowing that every single website you've visited and topic you've searched for in popular browsers such as Chrome and Safari has been collected and could be sold to advertisers?

Despite the almost nonexistent privacy regulations in the United States, there are some steps you can take to limit the amount of data collected when browsing the internet. First, disable cookies, and decline any cookie requests. While this can significantly reduce your digital footprint, opting out isn't always easy. And when using traditional websites, it's almost impossible not to accumulate cookies, so get into the habit of clearing your cache and cookies regularly. Also, frequently delete your browsing history. If privacy is a priority, consider downloading a VPN, such as Hot Spot Shield.

## Privacy Settings and Alerts

Most people don't take the time to examine, never mind change, the privacy settings on their various accounts. They just stick with the default. Why? It's easier.

If you use Instagram, Twitter, Facebook, LinkedIn, or any other popular social media site, it's worth taking a few minutes to review the choices, especially if you share sensitive informa-tion. Social media account settings can determine who can see your posts and if online activity on third-party sites is shared publicly. It puts you in control of what you want to share.

Regarding financial accounts, it's a good idea to sign up for push notifications to alert you of any banking or credit card transactions. This way, you will receive alerts for every ATM withdrawal or purchase and can immediately identify any fraudulent activity. Some companies let you place additional safeguards and protections on your financial accounts. One example is Wells Fargo, which lets you set up voice verification, so nobody pretending to be you can call up and gain access to your account.

## Lock Your Devices

I know how annoying it is to punch in the passcode every time you want to open your iPhone or computer; this is why people don't use passcodes. But I promise, after a few days, you won't even notice it anymore. And the benefits far outweigh the potential cost.

Instead of a four- or six-digit code, consider using biometric passcodes, such as Face ID, Touch ID, facial recognition, and fingerprint scans, because they add an additional layer of security. If you lose your phone, or it gets stolen, and a passcode isn't required to access it, you're essentially handing over your phone, text messages, email, social media, and financial accounts to whoever has the phone.

## Update Your Software

Many people cringe when they see that their software has to be updated because it means they have to stop what they're doing at some point and wait for their systems to update. Sometimes it's quick and painless, and sometimes it takes a little longer than expected.

Hackers exploit the bugs and weaknesses in the software on your computer and phone. New software updates can patch up these vulnerabilities to keep your system secure. Whether it's your operating system, browser, or antivirus software, take the time to update it when you get an alert; it's well worth it. And turn on automatic updates when possible, so you don't have to worry about doing it manually. Don't even give yourself a choice.

## Dealing with Spam

By now, you know better than to click on suspicious links from unknown senders, but what happens if you do so by accident?

We scroll so quickly that clicking on one of these links is easy. It happens, but what does that mean? Are you suddenly at risk? Did all of those precautionary measures you took go out the window because you accidentally clicked on a phishing link while trying to delete it or close out the window? Short answer: No! Long answer: It kind of depends.

If you have clicked on phishing links or downloaded suspicious files or email attachments, you immediately want to disconnect from your network, backup your files, scan your device for malware, and then change your passwords.

## Don't Ignore Security Alerts

This includes any emails about failed login attempts or attempts to change the password of any existing accounts.

This is an early indication of a hacking attempt and paying attention to these alerts is a simple way to safeguard your accounts. However, there is a catch!

Hackers use your own fear of being hacked against you and often try to use these emails in phishing attacks. That's why you never want to click a link or scan a QR code to sign into any of your accounts because that link will redirect you to a site that looks eerily similar to the legitimate one but is not at all authentic. You will then be instructed to sign into your account, but what's really happening is that thieves are scooping up your login credentials to take over your account.

Before you take any action, make sure the alert is legitimate. Look for red flags, like misspelled company or platform names. If you receive an email, it should always come from the official website. If you still can't tell, it's best to contact the company directly to inquire about any issues with your account.

## Keeping Sensitive Documents Secure

Real-world protection and healthy security habits are just as important as digital habits. You know how disastrous losing your wallet can be. Not only do you have to replace all your cards and documents, but your driver's license, credit cards, and debit cards give criminals all the information they need to commit financial fraud and identity theft.

Protect yourself by carrying around only the documents you need. That means leaving your Social Security card at home and in a secure location along with your birth certificate, passport, green card, checks, bank statements, and any unused credit cards.

A good way to limit the number of sensitive documents you have in your home is by going paperless. By signing up for online billing and getting digital statements, that's one less document with your account information that thieves can get their hands on. Keep in mind that mail fraud is becoming more common. This can be an issue depending on how accessible your mailbox is to the public. It's good to get in the habit of collecting the mail daily and putting a hold on it if you'll be away for an extended period.

All of this sounds good in theory, but sometimes it's unavoidable. Mail can pile up, and it's not always possible to go paperless. In that case, you want to shred all documents containing sensitive personal or financial information. This includes bank statements, credit card statements, pay stubs, and medical bills. Also, destroy any old credit or debit cards. You don't want to leave those lying around.

## Before You Download

Free apps and mobile games are enticing, but if you're downloading them from third-party sources, there's a good chance they might contain malware. According to Aura's survey conducted online by the Harris Poll, 40 percent of Americans admit to downloading apps, software, or files from third-party sources.[5] Only download apps from trusted sources, such as the Apple Store and Google Play. Even those aren't all guaranteed to be legitimate, but they do the best job of filtering out the junk.

## Helpful Resources

- **Free dark web scan:** It can be frightening to think what information of yours might be out there. That's why Aura offers a free dark web scan at our website. Just go to the site and see if your personal data has been exposed or if there are any passwords associated with your email address that have been leaked.
- **Scam tracker:** If you, your parents, or your kids come across an offer or get a message that you fear might be a scam, but aren't sure, check with the BBB Scam Tracker. On this site, you can search for existing scams or report offers to be investigated.
- **Google alerts:** Do you want to know when your name appears online? Sign up for a Google Alert that will notify you if any of the information you are tracking appears online. This lets you see how your online footprint might be growing and delete any unwanted mentions.

# Conclusion

# Getting One Step Ahead of Cybercrime

There is a sense today that cybercriminals have become part of the family. They've seen the pictures you've posted, can peruse your search history, learn your Social Security number, and with enough resources and data, can actually take over your digital identity to become you! They can cost you your money, reputation, and security. And no matter how much you want them gone, they aren't going away on their own—but you have the power to liberate yourself.

Once the behaviors that comprise healthy digital safety habits have been instilled in your family members, digital safety shifts into autopilot. You can begin decreasing your digital footprint. You know what to look for and can better identify a scam or a digital anomaly before becoming a victim. If something slips through the cracks, you know what to do.

I know this can be overwhelming and it's a lot to remember. Nobody is perfect. People cut corners and make mistakes. It's human nature, and you can't be faulted for that, but you don't want one of those mistakes to come back to bite you, which is why you can take your protections one step further.

Digital safety tools such as intelligent safety can make this process even easier because it puts the power of artificial intelligence in your corner. While it's great to be notified of fraud, isn't it much better to prevent it from ever occurring? Given how interconnected digital threats are today, and how your behavior on one platform could impact your safety on another, you want protection that is also interconnected. The internet is a network, security should be as well. Proactive protection puts you a step ahead of cybercriminals, not one step behind like you are when forced to react to alerts. Your family's personal, financial, and health information is only as strong as your weakest link. Intelligent safety shores up all of your family's digital vulnerabilities, so you don't have to worry about it.

It's been a long journey, but I'm so proud of what our team at Aura has created and accomplished in such a short period of time. We've taken that difficult but necessary first step of putting the power back in the hands of the consumer, and I've enjoyed watching that dream of creating an integrated form of digital safety come to fruition. Challenges still remain, but given the possibilities and advancements that can be made using intelligent safety, I also know that we're only getting started. Unlike when I was first hacked back in 2014, I can now see a path forward to a much safer internet. I invite you to join me on that road and rest assured knowing that you're doing what's needed to protect your family's data, finances, security, and future.

# Notes

## Foreword: The Next Big Thing in Digital Safety

1. Staff, the Premerger Notification Office, and DPIP and CTO Staff. "Consumer Sentinel Network Data Book 2020." Federal Trade Commission, August 24, 2021.
2. "Burglary." FBI. FBI, September 12, 2019. https://ucr.fbi.gov/crime -in-the-u.s/2019/crime-in-the-u.s.-2019/topic-pages/burglary.
3. "IC3 Annual Report—2021 Internet Crime Report." PSA Computer Services, June 24, 2022. https://psa-2.com/ic3-annual-report-2021 -internet-crime-report/.

## Part 1: How Intelligent Safety Can Stop Big Cybercrime

1. "U.S. Consumers and Cyber Crime." Statista Research Department, July 6, 2022. https://www.statista.com/topics/2588/us-consumers-and -cyber-crime/#dossierContents__outerWrapper.
2. "IC3 Annual Report—2021 Internet Crime Report." PSA Computer Services, June 24, 2022. https://psa-2.com/ic3-annual-report-2021 -internet-crime-report/.
3. Britt, Phil, Joan Engebretson, and Carl Weinschenk. "Report: Connected Devices Have More than Doubled since 2019." Telecompetitor, June 9, 2021. https://www.telecompetitor.com/report-connected -devices-have-more-than-doubled-since-2019/.

## Chapter 1: The Business of Cybercrime

1. "2022 Cyber Security Statistics Trends & Data." PurpleSec, 2022, https://purplesec.us/resources/cyber-security-statistics/#Cybercrime.

2. Staff, the Premerger Notification Office, and DPIP and CTO Staff. "Consumer Sentinel Network Data Book 2021." Federal Trade Commission, https://www.ftc.gov/system/files/ftc_gov/pdf/CSN%20Annual%20Data%20Book%202021%20Final%20PDF.pdf.

3. Rosemarie, Kira. "Medical Identity Theft." Debt.com, LLC, 2022. https://www.debt.com/identity-theft/medical/.

4. "United States Department of Labor." Office of Inspector General—U.S. Department of Labor—About OIG. September 22, 2022. https://www.oig.dol.gov/doloiguioversightwork.htm.

5. Smith, Bridie, and Reid Sexton. "Three Australians Shocked by ID Theft." *Sydney Morning Herald*, February 25, 2010. https://www.smh.com.au/national/three-australians-shocked-by-id-theft-20100225-p5zj.html.

6. "Taxpayers Whose Legitimate Returns Are Flagged by IRS Fraud Filters . . ." Annual Report to Congress 2020. Taxpayer Advocate Service. https://www.taxpayeradvocate.irs.gov/wp-content/uploads/2021/01/ARC20_MSP_10_RefundDelays.pdf.

7. "2021 Annual Report," Identity Theft Tax Refund Fraud Sharing and Analysis Center. https://www.irs.gov/pub/newsroom/2021-isac-annual-report.pdf.

8. Einhorn, Erin, and Aaron Mondry. "The 'Fake Landlord' Scam Destroys Lives in Detroit. But Culprits Rarely Face Consequences." NBCNews.com, November 10, 2021. https://www.nbcnews.com/news/us-news/fake-landlord-home-rental-scam-detroit-rcna4941.

9. "$1 Billion in Losses Reported by Victims of Romance Scams." FBI, February 10, 2022. https://www.fbi.gov/contact-us/field-offices/houston/news/press-releases/1-billion-in-losses-reported-by-victims-of-romance-scams.

10. Anderson, Monica, Emily A. Vogles, and Erica Turner. "The Virtues and Downsides of Online Dating." Pew Research Center, February 6, 2020. https://www.pewresearch.org/internet/2020/02/06/the-virtues-and-downsides-of-online-dating/.

11. Britnell, Lanny. "The Changing Face of Identity Theft—Federal Trade Commission." https://www.ftc.gov/sites/default/files/documents/public

_comments/credit-report-freezes-534030-00033/534030–00033 .pdf.

12. Staff, the Premerger Notification Office, and DPIP and CTO Staff. "Consumer Sentinel Network Data Book 2021." Federal Trade Commission, https://www.ftc.gov/system/files/ftc_gov/pdf/CSN %20Annual%20Data%20Book%202021%20Final%20PDF.pdf.

13. "AARP Survey: Veterans More Likely to Lose Money to Scams than Civilians." MediaRoom, November 9, 2021. https://press.aarp.org /2021-11-9-AARP-Survey-Veterans-More-Likely-to-Lose-Money -to-Scams-Than-Civilians.

14. Galov, Nick. "17+ Sinister Social Engineering Statistics for 2022." WebTribunal, October 15, 2022. https://webtribunal.net/blog/social -engineering-statistics/#gref.

15. "Federal Bureau of Investigation Internet Crime Report 2021, "Internet Crime Complaint Center(ic3): FBI and IC3. https://www .ic3.gov/Home/AnnualReports.

16. Kaplan, Michael. "'Baby Al Capone' Ellis Pinsky Teams with Alleged Crypto-Crime Victim to Take on AT&T." *New York Post*, October 21, 2022. https://nypost.com/2022/10/20/ellis-pinsky-teams-with -alleged-victim-michael-terpin-to-take-on-att/.

17. BlockchainJournal. "A Cryptocurrency Investor Received $ 75.8 Million of Compensation in a Sim Fake Case." ESP Blockchain Journal, May 13, 2019. https://blockchainjournal.news/es/a-crypto currency-investor-received-75-8-million-of-compensation-in-a-sim -fake-case/.

18. "A Pandemic on Mobile: Mobile AD Fraud 2021 Report." Secure-D. 2022. https://www.secure-d.io/mobileadfraud2021report/.

19. Wagenseil, Paul. "More than 1,200 Iphone Apps Infected with Malware—What You Need to Know." Tom's Guide. August 25, 2020. https://www.tomsguide.com/news/iphone-apps-infected-malware.

20. Phillips, Jamie. "Mother's Horror at Hearing Creepy Man 'Shushing' Two-Year-Old Son through Baby Monitor." *Daily Mail*, February 16, 2022. https://www.dailymail.co.uk/news/article-10518765/Mothers -horror-hearing-creepy-man-shushing-two-year-old-son-baby -monitor.html.

## Chapter 2: The Information Economy Fueling the Fire

1. Duhigg, Charles. "How Companies Learn Your Secrets." *New York Times*, February 16, 2012. https://www.nytimes.com/2012/02/19/magazine /shopping-habits.html?pagewanted=1&_r=1&hp.

2. St. John, Paige. "The Untold Story of How the Golden State Killer Was Found: A Covert Operation and Private DNA." *Los Angeles Times*, December 8, 2020. https://www.latimes.com/california/story /2020-12-08/man-in-the-window#:~:text=The%20dramatic%20 arrest%20in%202018,to%20trace%20their%20family%20trees.

3. "Whistleblower Reveals Info on Companies Buying and Selling Your Location Data." CBS News, April 29, 2019. https://www.cbsnews .com/news/location-tracking-whistleblower-reveals-info-on-companies -buying-and-selling-your-location-data/.

4. "SuperAwesome Launches Kid-Safe Filter to Prevent Online Ads from Stealing Children's Personal Data." SuperAwesome, December 6, 2018. https://www.superawesome.com/superawesome-launches-kid -safe-filter-to-prevent-online-ads-from-stealing-childrens-personal -data/.

5. Bischoff, Paul. "1 In 5 Children's Google Play Apps Breach Children's Online Privacy Protection Act Rules." Comparitech, June 22, 2021. https://www.comparitech.com/blog/vpn-privacy/app-coppa-study/.

## Chapter 3: What's Really at Stake?

1. Poulson, Kevin, Robert McMillan, and Melanie Evans. "A Hospital Hit by Hackers, a Baby in Distress: The Case of the First Alleged Ransomware Death." *Wall Street Journal*, September 30, 2021. https://www.wsj.com/articles/ransomware-hackers-hospital-first -alleged-death-11633008116?mod=hp_lead_pos5.

2. "Ponemon Research Report: The Impact of Ransomware on Healthcare during COVID-19 and Beyond." Censinet. https://www .censinet.com/ponemon-report-covid-impact-ransomware.

3. Jercich, Kat. "Ponemon Study Finds Link between Ransomware, Increased Mortality Rate." Healthcare IT News, September 22, 2021. https://www.healthcareitnews.com/news/ponemon-study-finds -link-between-ransomware-increased-mortality-rate.

4. Page, Carly. "Hackers Leak 500GB Trove of Data Stolen during LAUSD Ransomware Attack." TechCrunch, October 3, 2022. https://techcrunch.com/2022/10/03/los-angeles-school-district-ransomware-data/?guccounter=1&guce_referrer=aHR0cHM6Ly93d3cuZ29vZ2xlLmNvbS88&guce_referrer_sig=AQAAAMeG6exwhhr2UmnbBm6ntvhu1VURTpL5vHemAAtVuVvgMzFNJjgeRDoF4UhQ0HP4u0FEbc2IF_U5lz9MEaURQdTWEKaxNztirxIiRnf0at6OeBUhG_GsV1fvAo9Be2VWqteACcNQfgQTnVRAkPNWYMN27oKSau5bexThlNYvdfeD.

5. Bischoff, Paul. "Ransomware Attacks on US Schools and Colleges Cost $3.56bn in 2021." Comparitech, June 23, 2022. https://www.comparitech.com/blog/information-security/school-ransomware-attacks/.

6. Staff, the Premerger Notification Office, and DPIP and CTO Staff. "Consumer Sentinel Network Data Book 2021." Federal Trade Commission, https://www.ftc.gov/system/files/ftc_gov/pdf/CSN%20Annual%20Data%20Book%202021%20Final%20PDF.pdf.

7. "2021 Consumer Aftermath Report: How Identity Crimes Impact Victims, Their Families, Friends, and . . .—ITRC." Identity Theft Resource Center. https://www.idtheftcenter.org/wp-content/uploads/2021/09/ITRC_2021_Consumer_Aftermath_Report.pdf.

8. "Identity Theft Resource Center's 2021 Annual Data Breach Report Sets New Record for Number of Compromises." ITRC, January 24, 2022. https://www.idtheftcenter.org/post/identity-theft-resource-center-2021-annual-data-breach-report-sets-new-record-for-number-of-compromises/.

9. Statler, Jason. "New Report: How Data Breaches Fuel Cyber Crime for the Whole Family—F-Secure Blog." F-Secure, February 9, 2021. https://blog.f-secure.com/the-walking-breached/.

10. Ibid.

11. Avan-Nomayo, Osato. "Ledger Data Leak: A 'Simple Mistake' Exposed 270k Crypto Wallet Buyers." Cointelegraph, December 24, 2020. https://cointelegraph.com/news/ledger-data-leak-a-simple-mistake-exposed-270k-crypto-wallet-buyers.

12. Cluley, Graham. "Fake Ledger Devices Mailed out in Attempt to Steal from Cryptocurrency Fans." Bitdefender, June 17, 2021. https://www.bitdefender.com/blog/hotforsecurity/fake-ledger-devices-mailed-out-in-attempt-to-steal-from-cryptocurrency-fans.

13. Varga, Gergo. "The Gen-Z Fraud Report: Young Americans & Fraud." SEON, May 19, 2022. https://seon.io/resources/gen-z-report-online-fraud/.

14. "Truecaller Insights 2022 U.S. Spam & Scam Report." *Truecaller*, May 24, 2022. https://www.truecaller.com/blog/insights/truecaller-insights-2022-us-spam-scam-report.

15. Ball, James. "Mugged for My Phone, Then Locked out of My Life." *Sunday Times*, June 26, 2022. https://www.thetimes.co.uk/article/mugged-for-my-phone-then-locked-out-of-my-life-92kpv50x7.

16. Harrell , Erika. "Victims of Identity Theft 2018." U.S. Department of Justice, April 2021. https://bjs.ojp.gov/content/pub/pdf/vit18.pdf.

17. "How Online Identity Fraud Destroyed One Man's Life." Private WiFi, November 15, 2010. https://blog.privatewifi.com/how-identity-fraud-destroyed-one-man%E2%80%99s-life/.

18. "Mobile Theft & Loss Report 2020." Prey. Accessed November 25, 2022. https://preyproject.com/resources/ebooks/mobile-theft-report-2020.

19. "Financial Fraud Crime Victims." The United States Department of Justice. The United States Attorney's Office Western District of Washington, February 10, 2015. https://www.justice.gov/usao-wdwa/victim-witness/victim-info/financial-fraud.

20. "New Study by Identity Theft Resource Center® Explores the Non-Economic Negative Impacts Caused by Identity Theft." ITRC, October 18, 2018. https://www.idtheftcenter.org/post/new-study-by-identity-theft-resource-center-explores-the-non-economic-negative-impacts-caused-by-identity-theft/.

## Chapter 4: The Data Privacy Movement

1. Hartzog, Woodrow, and Daniel J. Solove. "We Still Haven't Learned the Major Lesson of the 2013 Target Hack." *Slate*, April 13, 2022.

https://slate.com/technology/2022/04/breached-excerpt-hartzog -solove-target.html.

2. "30 Biggest GDPR Fines to-Date: Latest GDPR Fines: Updated 2022." Tessian, May 5, 2022. https://www.tessian.com/blog/biggest -gdpr-fines-2020/#:~:text=The%20EU%20General%20Data%20 Protection,financial%20year%20%E2%80%93%20whichever%20 is%20higher.

3. "Marketing Company Agrees to Pay $150 Million for Facilitating Elder Fraud Schemes." United States Department of Justice, January 27, 2021. https://www.justice.gov/opa/pr/marketing-company-agrees -pay-150-million-facilitating-elder-fraud-schemes.

4. Keegan, Jon, and Alfred Ng. "The Popular Family Safety App Life360 Is Selling Precise Location Data on Its Tens of Millions of Users." The Markup, December 6, 2021. https://themarkup.org /privacy/2021/12/06/the-popular-family-safety-app-life360-is-selling -precise-location-data-on-its-tens-of-millions-of-user.

5. Neely, Amber. "Life360 To Stop Selling Precise Location Data of Users." AppleInsider, January 28, 2022. https://appleinsider.com /articles/22/01/28/life360-to-stop-selling-precise-location-data -of-users#:~:text=Life360%20has%20decided%20to%20 stop,users%27%20data%20in%20aggregate%20form.

6. "Gen Z and Millennials Less Serious about Cybersecurity on Work-Issued Devices than Personal, According to New EY Consulting Survey." EY, October 18, 2022. https://www.prnewswire.com/news -releases/gen-z-and-millennials-less-serious-about-cybersecurity -on-work-issued-devices-than-personal-according-to-new-ey-consulting -survey-301649378.html.

7. Osterman Research. https://ostermanresearch.com/.

8. "Cost of a Data Breach 2022." IBM, 2022. https://www.ibm.com /reports/data-breach.

9. Shein, Esther. "667% Spike in Email Phishing Attacks Due to Coronavirus Fears." TechRepublic, March 26, 2020. https://www .techrepublic.com/article/667-spike-in-email-phishing-attacks-due -to-coronavirus-fears/.

10. Jain, Khushbu, and Brijesh Singh. "Here's How to Browse Your Way through Phishing, Cyber Threats as You Work from Home during Covid-19." News18, April 9, 2020. https://www.news18.com/news /opinion/heres-how-to-browse-your-way-through-phishing-cyber -threats-as-you-work-from-home-during-covid-19-2564969.html.

11. Krebs, Brian. "Glut of Fake LinkedIn Profiles Pits HR against the Bots." Krebs on Security, October 5, 2022. https://krebsonsecurity.com /2022/10/glut-of-fake-linkedin-profiles-pits-hr-against-the-bots/.

12. "Majority of Businesses Still Have Remote Working Cybersecurity Concerns One Year into the Pandemic, Finds Thales." Thales, June 2, 2021. https://cpl.thalesgroup.com/about-us/news-room/cyber -security-concerns.

13. Emerman, Ed. "Pandemic Accelerates Employer Voluntary Benefit Offerings, Willis Towers Watson Survey Finds." Willis Towers Watson, May 13, 2021. https://www.wtwco.com/en-US /News/2021/05/pandemic-accelerates-employer-voluntary-benefit -offerings-wtw-survey-finds.

14. "The Impacts of Identity Theft on Employees and Their Workplace— ITRC." Identity Theft Resource Center. https://www.idtheftcenter .org/wp-content/uploads/2020/08/Identity-Theft-in-the-Workplace -Aura-ITRC-Report-081420-WEB-ADA.pdf.

15. Ibid.

## Chapter 5: A New Paradigm: Intelligent Safety

1. "Identity Fraud Losses Increase 15 Percent as Consumer Out-of -Pocket Costs More than Double, According to 2020 Identity Fraud Report." Javelin, May 13, 2020. https://javelinstrategy.com/press -release/identity-fraud-losses-increase-15-percent-consumer-out -pocket-costs-more-double.

2. "Psychology of Passwords: The Online Behavior That's . . ." LastPass by LogMeIn, 2020. https://lp-cdn.lastpass.com/lporcamedia /document-library/lastpass/pdf/en/LastPass-B2C-Assets-Ebook.pdf.

3. "Infographics—Screen Time vs. Lean Time." Centers for Disease Control and Prevention, January 29, 2018. https://www.cdc.gov /nccdphp/dnpao/multimedia/infographics/getmoving.html.

## Part 2: Protecting Your Connected Family

1. "Federal Bureau of Investigation Internet Crime Report 2021," Internet Crime Complaint Center(ic3): FBI and IC3. https://www.ic3.gov/Home/AnnualReports.

## Chapter 6: The Secret Lives (And Risks) of Connected Kids

1. "Connected Families: How Parents Think and Feel about Wearables, Toys, and the Internet of Things." Family Online Safety Institute, 2017. https://www.fosi.org/.
2. Turner, Terry. "Internet Safety for Kids: Parents' Guide to Keeping Kids Safe Online." Consumer Notice, LLC, July 12, 2022. https://www.consumernotice.org/data-protection/internet-safety-for-kids/.
3. Auxier, Brooke, Monica Anderson, Andrew Perrin, and Erica Turner. "Parenting Approaches and Concerns Related to Digital Devices." Pew Research Center: Internet, Science & Tech. Pew Research Center, July 28, 2020. https://www.pewresearch.org/internet/2020/07/28/parenting-approaches-and-concerns-related-to-digital-devices/.
4. Varanasi, Lakshmi. "Gen Z Is Increasingly Using TikTok Videos Instead of Google Search, but 1 in 5 of Them Contain Misinformation, a New Study Says." Business Insider, September 19, 2022. https://www.businessinsider.com/gen-z-uses-tiktok-over-google-but-videos-contain-misinformation-2022-9.
5. Vogels, Emily A., Risa Gelles-Watnick, and Navid Massarat. "Teens, Social Media and Technology 2022." Pew Research Center: Internet, Science & Tech, August 10, 2022. https://www.pewresearch.org/internet/2022/08/10/teens-social-media-and-technology-2022/?utm_content=null&utm_source=Sailthru&utm_medium=email&utm_campaign=Thursday+Email&utm_term=4ABCD.
6. Dvorak, Chyelle. "What Data Does TikTok Collect?" Reviews.org, February 22, 2022. https://www.reviews.org/internet-service/what-data-does-tiktok-collect/.
7. Fung, Brian. "UK Could Fine Tiktok $29 Million over Children's Privacy Concerns | CNN Business." CNN, September 26, 2022. https://www.cnn.com/2022/09/26/tech/uk-tiktok-fine/index.html.

8. "Federal Bureau of Investigation Internet Crime Report 2021," Internet Crime Complaint Center(ic3): FBI and IC3. https://www .ic3.gov/Home/AnnualReports.

9. Huddleston, Tom. "Kids Today Are 'Overly Confident' about Their Skills Online-Losing $101.4 Million to Hackers Last Year." CNBC, October 27, 2022. https://www.cnbc.com/2022/10/26/kids-lose-millions-online-to-hackers-social-catfish-report-fbi-data.html ?utm_campaign=itb&utm_medium=newsletter&utm _source=morning_brew.

10. "Snapchat Support." Snapchat. https://support.snapchat.com/en-US /a/password-sharing.

11. "Children and Grooming / Online Predators." Child Crime Prevention & Safety Center, 2022. https://childsafety.losangeles criminallawyer.pro/children-and-grooming-online-predators.html.

12. "Responding to Online Threats: Minors' Perspectives." Thorn. Benenson Strategy Group, May 2021. https://info.thorn.org/hubfs /Research/Responding%20to%20Online%20Threats_2021-Full -Report.pdf.

13. https://www.businesswire.com/news/home/20211102005484/en /Child-Identity-Fraud-Costs-Nearly-1-Billion-Annually-According -to-a-New-Study-From-Javelin-Strategy-Research.

14. https://www.pewresearch.org/internet/2022/08/10/teens-social-media -and-technology-2022/?utm_content=null&utm_source=Sailthru &utm_medium=email&utm_campaign=Thursday%20 Email&utm_term=4ABCD.

15. "Circle's Parent Guide to the Most Popular Video Games." Circle, September 12, 2021. https://meetcircle.com/blogs/stories /parent-guide-to-video-games.

16. Paul, Kari. "Twitch Hack: Data Breach Exposes Sensitive Information." *The Guardian*, October 6, 2021. https://www.theguardian.com /technology/2021/oct/06/twitch-hack-data-breach-gaming-platform.

17. Kaspersky. "84% Of Parents Are Worried about Their Child's Online Safety, but Aren't Taking the Time to Talk about It." www.kasper sky.com, September 16, 2019. https://www.kaspersky.com/about /press-releases/2019_parents-are-worried-about-their-childs-online -safety.

18. "Parenting Teens in the Age of Social Media." Lurie Children's, September 1, 2020. https://www.luriechildrens.org/en/blog/social-media-parenting-statistics/.

19. Gordon, Sherri. "How to Handle Finding Disturbing Content on Your Teen's Phone." Verywell Family, July 27, 2021. https://www.verywellfamily.com/disturbing-content-on-childs-phone-4582426.

20. Auxier, Brooke, Monica Anderson, Andrew Perrin, and Erica Turner. "Parental Views about YouTube." Pew Research Center: Internet, Science & Tech. Pew Research Center, July 28, 2020. https://www.pewresearch.org/internet/2020/07/28/parental-views-about-youtube/.

21. "Child Safety." Apple, 2022. https://www.apple.com/child-safety/.

22. Patchin, Justin W. "Cyberbullying Data 2019." Cyberbullying Research Center, July 9, 2019. https://cyberbullying.org/2019-cyberbullying-data.

23. Anderson, Monica. "A Majority of Teens Have Experienced Some Form of Cyberbullying." Pew Research Center: Internet, Science & Tech, September 27, 2018. https://www.pewresearch.org/internet/2018/09/27/a-majority-of-teens-have-experienced-some-form-of-cyberbullying/.

24. "Cyberbullying: Spotting the Signs and Helping Children and Teenagers Handle It." Raising Children Network, March 15, 2022. https://raisingchildren.net.au/pre-teens/behaviour/bullying/cyberbullying-helping-your-child#getrid-steps-helping-children-and-teenagers-handle-cyberbullying-nav-title.

25. "Federal Bureau of Investigation Internet Crime Report 2021," Internet Crime Complaint Center(ic3): FBI and IC3. https://www.ic3.gov/Home/AnnualReports.

26. Campbell, Josh, and Jason Kravarik. "A 17-Year-Old Boy Died by Suicide Hours after Being Scammed. The FBI Says It's Part of a Troubling Increase in 'Sextortion' Cases." CNN, May 23, 2022. https://www.cnn.com/2022/05/20/us/ryan-last-suicide-sextortion-california/index.html.

27. Anwar, Hura. "Young Children Are Losing One Full Night's Sleep Each Week Due to Social Media, Claims New Study." Digital Information World, September 22, 2022. https://www.digitalin

formationworld.com/2022/09/young-children-are-losing-one-full .html?m=1.

28. Staff, the Premerger Notification Office, and DPIP and CTO Staff. "Consumer Sentinel Network Data Book 2021." Federal Trade Commission, https://www.ftc.gov/system/files/ftc_gov/pdf /CSN%20Annual%20Data%20Book%202021%20Final%20PDF .pdf.

29. Kitten, Tracy. "Child Identity Fraud: The Perils of Too Many Screens and Social Media." Javelin, October 26, 2022. https://javelinstrategy. com/2022-child-identity-fraud-report.

30. Kitten, Tracy. "Child Identity Fraud: A Web of Deception and Loss." Javelin, November 2, 2021. https://javelinstrategy.com/research/child -identity-fraud-web-deception-and-loss.

31. "Child Identity Fraud Costs Nearly $1 Billion Annually, According to a New Study from Javelin Strategy & Research." Javelin, November 2, 2021. https://javelinstrategy.com/press-release/child -identity-fraud-costs-nearly-1-billion-annually-according-new -study-javelin.

32. Ibid.

33. "Child Identity Fraud: A Web of Deception and Loss." Javelin's 2023 financial trends and predictions. Escalent, November 2021. https: //javelinstrategy.com/.

## Chapter 7: Scammers versus Your Aging Parents

1. "Two Women Sentenced in Multi-Million-Dollar Medicare Fraud Scheme." United States Department of Justice, February 15, 2022. https://www.justice.gov/usao-ma/pr/two-women-sentenced -multi-million-dollar-medicare-fraud-scheme.

2. "Colombian National Pleads Guilty to $109 Million Medicare Fraud Scheme." The United States Department of Justice, October 29, 2020. https://www.justice.gov/usao-ma/pr/colombian-national -pleads-guilty-109-million-medicare-fraud-scheme.

3. Rosemarie, Kira. "Medical Identity Theft." Debt.com, LLC, November 10, 2022. https://www.debt.com/identity-theft/medical/.

4. Finnegan, Joanne. "Doctors Must Fight for Their Innocence in Fraud Cases, Say Defense Attorneys." Fierce Healthcare, March 5, 2018.

https://www.fiercehealthcare.com/practices/doctors-innocence -healthcare-fraud-pramela-ganji.

5. "Largest Healthcare Data Breaches of 2021." HIPAA Journal, December 30, 2021. https://www.hipaajournal.com/largest-healthcare -data-breaches-of-2021/.

6. "Reporting Medicare Fraud & Abuse." Medicare, 2022. https: //www.medicare.gov/basics/reporting-medicare-fraud-and-abuse.

7. "Physician Indicted in $6 Million Medicare Fraud Scheme." United States Department of Justice, May 7, 2021. https://www.justice.gov /opa/pr/physician-indicted-6-million-medicare-fraud-scheme.

8. "Get the Facts on Elder Abuse." National Council on Aging, February 23, 2021. https://www.ncoa.org/article/get-the-facts-on-elder-abuse.

9. Weiss, Gary."How to Protect Yourself from Family Fraud." AARP, February 1, 2018. https://www.aarp.org/money/scams-fraud/info -2018/family-fraud.html.

10. "Elder Fraud Report 2020." FBI. Internet Crime Complaint Center, 2020. https://www.ic3.gov/media/pdf/annualreport/2020_ic3report .pdf.

11. Karimi, Faith. "An 80-Year-Old Widower Lost $200,000 in an Online Romance Scam in Oregon." CNN, February 14, 2020. https://edition.cnn.com/2020/02/14/us/happy-valentines-dont-fall -for-romance-scams-trnd/index.html.

## Chapter 8: Protecting Your Family Finances

1. "FTC Sends More than $11m in Refunds to Consumers Affected by Credit Card Interest Rate Reduction Scam." Federal Trade Commission, April 28, 2021. https://www.ftc.gov/news-events /news/press-releases/2021/04/ftc-sends-more-11m-refunds-consumers -affected-credit-card-interest-rate-reduction-scam.

2. "Aura Survey Reveals 7 in 10 Veterans and Active-Duty Service Members Have Experienced Digital Crime." Aura, 2022. https: //press.aura.com/2022-11-11-Aura-Survey-reveals-7-in-10-Veterans -and-Active-Duty-Service-Members-Have-Experienced-Digital -Crime.

3. Ibid.

4. "Federal Bureau of Investigation Internet Crime Report 2021," Internet Crime Complaint Center(ic3): FBI and IC3. https://www.ic3.gov/Home/AnnualReports.

5. "Online Shopping Fraud Study." Better Business Bureau, 2022. https://www.bbb.org/all/scamstudies/fake_online_retailers_study/online_shopping_fraud_study.

6. "Online Purchase Scams 2021: BBB Institute for Marketplace Trust." Better Business Bureau, 2022. https://www.bbb.org/all/bbbi/online-purchase-scams-2021.

7. "Breaking Down Phishing Site TLDs and Certificate Abuse in Q1." PhishLabs, June 24, 2021. https://www.phishlabs.com/blog/breaking-down-phishing-site-tlds-and-certificate-abuse-in-q1/.

8. Knowles, Jason, and Ann Pistone. "Bank Account Fraud, Hacking Causes Customers to Lose Hundreds of Dollars." ABC7 Chicago, March 7, 2022. https://abc7chicago.com/bank-account-fraud-theft-online/11629312/.

9. "Online Shopping Fraud Study." Better Business Bureau, 2022. https://www.bbb.org/all/scamstudies/fake_online_retailers_study/online_shopping_fraud_study.

## Chapter 9: Nurturing Healthy Digital Safety Habits

1. Buchholz, Katharina. "The Most Popular Passwords around the World." Statista Infographics, February 9, 2021. https://www.statista.com/chart/16922/most-popular-passwords-2017-and-2018/.

2. Buchholz, Katharina. "How Safe Is Your Password?" Statista Infographics, December 1, 2021. https://www.statista.com/chart/26298/time-it-would-take-a-computer-to-crack-a-password/.

3. Fowler, Geoffrey A. "She Clicked Sign-in with Google. Strangers Got Access to All Her Files." *Washington Post*, October 24, 2022. https://www.washingtonpost.com/technology/2022/10/21/sign-in-google-facebook/.

4. Sabin, Sam. "Meta Detects More than 400 Mobile Apps Stealing Facebook Passwords." Axios, October 7, 2022. https://www.axios.com/2022/10/07/meta-400-mobile-apps-facebook-user-passwords.

5.  "Cybersecurity Awareness Month: Nine Online Behaviors Putting You at Risk." Aura, 2022. https://press.aura.com/2021-10-20 -Cybersecurity-Awareness-Month-Nine-Online-Behaviors-Putting -You-At-Risk.

# Index

# About the Author

Hari Ravichandran has had an entrepreneurial spirit since he was a kid growing up in India. His father desperately wanted him to build a better future for himself, and at fifteen, he earned a scholarship to live with an American host family and attend high school. He then defied the odds and earned his ticket to stay in the United States when he was accepted to college. He studied engineering and always loved technology, so at twenty, in true Silicon Valley style, he started a web hosting company out of his garage with his own capital and grew it into a publicly traded company with an enterprise value of approximately $3.5 billion and more than 3,500 employees worldwide. With an established track record of founding and investing in successful businesses in technology and security, Hari founded Aura in 2017 to simplify digital security for consumers. He has since grown Aura into a company valued at $2.5 billion, dedicated to creating a safer internet for everyone. Hari is named on over forty approved or pending technology patents, was named Ernst & Young's 2012 Entrepreneur of the Year (New England) and was also named to Forbes's list of "America's Most Powerful CEOs 40 and Under" in 2014 and 2015. He holds an MBA from the Wharton School at University of Pennsylvania and a BS in computer engineering from Mississippi State University.